COTTAGE LIVING

COTTAGE LIVING

Designing Comfortable Country Retreats

Ellen M. Plante

FRIEDMAN/FAIRFAX
PUBLISHERS

A FRIEDMAN/FAIRFAX BOOK

© 2000 by Michael Friedman Publishing Group, Inc.

Please visit our website: www.metrobooks.com

Library of Congress Cataloging-in-Publication Data

Plante, Ellen M.
    Cottage living : designing comfortable country retreats / Ellen M. Plante.
        p. cm.
    Includes index.
    ISBN 1-56799-979-4 (alk. paper)
    1. Decoration and ornament, Rustic--United States. 2. Cottages--United States. 3. Vacation homes--United States. I. Title.
    NK2002 .P59 2000
    747'.8837--dc21

                                                    00-037145

Editor: Hallie Einhorn
Art Director: Jeff Batzli
Designer: Kevin Ullrich
Photography Editor: Wendy Missan
Production Manager: Karen Matsu Greenberg

Color separations by Dai Nippon
Printed in Mexico

1 3 5 7 9 10 8 6 4 2

Distributed by Sterling Publishing Co., Inc.
387 Park Avenue South
New York, NY 10016-8810
Distributed in Canada by Sterling Publishing
Canadian Manda Group
One Atlantic Avenue, Suite 105
Toronto, Ontario, Canada M6K 3E7
Distributed in Australia by
Capricorn Link (Australia) Pty Ltd.
P.O. Box 6651
Baulkham Hills, Business Centre, NSW 2153, Australia

For my family, and all the trips to the mountains the future holds.

Special thanks to Hallie Einhorn,
my editor at Friedman/Fairfax Publishers.

Contents

Introduction

COTTAGE—SEVEN LITTLE LETTERS THAT WHEN COMBINED EVOKE IMAGES OF warmth and unsurpassable charm. Having almost universal appeal, the cottage conjures a feeling of quiet contentment, recalls sweet memories of summers past, and sparks a longing for a simple, scenic, and relaxing life—even if savored for just a short while.

The dictionary defines a cottage as a dwelling, though one that can take many forms. It is the small home of a peasant or farmer, a vacation retreat, or one of several buildings in a resort or camp. These dwellings, many of them in Europe centuries old, are closely linked to a certain lifestyle. And from this lifestyle a certain manner of decorating has emerged—one that is gracious yet unpretentious, free of any formal constraints. It is a style that affords a free-form approach to outfitting a snug and cozy home.

The cottage may be artfully cluttered or pared down and simple. Rooms may seem spacious, but are never too large. They may be chock-full of furniture and yet still seem enticingly intimate rather than crowded or overwhelming. In a single room, antiques and casual furnishings will blend harmoniously with flea market finds, favorite collections, and assorted memorabilia.

Cottages Past

Cottages, those homey retreats and gateways to personal happiness and self-expression, originated in response to a way of life closely tied to the land. The very word itself was derived from the Middle English word, *cote*, used to describe various huts or shelters for animals. Some of the earliest examples of cottages are the humble abodes built in England during the 1400s. These were constructed with readily available materials, such as stone, wood, and later brick. Roofs were typically made of thatch, slate, or tile.

Although these cozy medieval dwellings were initially occupied by servants, two centuries later cottages started popping up throughout the countryside as residences for farmers. Cottages also surfaced in small towns and villages, where they served as homes for shop owners and merchants. Most English cottages were one and a half or two stories high, with steeply pitched roofs and small, diamond-mullioned windows. Since glass initially had to be imported and continued to be quite costly once made in England, cottages generally retained their signature small windows throughout the eighteenth and nineteenth centuries.

Previous Page: *Stone walls provide character, while comfortable seating and splashes of color make this living room cozy and welcoming.*
Above: *Wide pine flooring, antique furniture, and textiles that evoke an earlier age recreate the past in this cottage bedroom. The colorful rug that sits next to the bed adds a whimsical touch.*

The cottage made its way to North America through European settlers. Along the Atlantic coast and in what were then known as Upper and Lower Canada, British colonists constructed small dwellings based on designs from the homeland, complete with thatched-straw roofs and, later, wooden shingles. In the Albany and Hudson River areas of New York State, the Dutch initially built small, one-story stone or wood houses with gambrel roofs and divided front doors (the earliest examples of what we refer to as Dutch Colonial

style). During the 1600s, Swedish settlers erected small log homes or cabins in the Delaware region, while in the 1700s German and Finnish immigrants put up small log homes in the Pennsylvania and Great Lakes areas. The French are noted for single-story homes combining a half-timber frame with stucco walls and pitched roofs. These vernacular French Colonial dwellings, concentrated in Mississippi and New Orleans, sported narrow windows complete with shutters as protection from the heat. And let's not forget the simple, straightforward Cape Cod cottage, which was really the first cottage style born in America. Arriving on the scene during the late eighteenth century, it went on to become an American architectural icon.

These early examples of cottages were practical and economical types of housing, which fulfilled the basic need for shelter while exhibiting a certain charm that has long been associated with small homes made of indigenous materials. Often built with an eye for the landscape and enhanced with small, informal gardens, these early cottages became the inspiration for ones built in the 1800s. Various social forces, including industrialization, the movement westward, and the rise of the middle class, led to an increase in cottages, which were built both as primary residences and as vacation homes throughout the nineteenth century. These later cottages may have manifested different architectural styles, but they retained key characteristics—namely a hearth as the home's focal point and small rooms for family intimacy—and thus maintained the ambience and basic ideology of their predecessors.

The meaning of "cottage" became more expansive during the Victorian era (1840 through the onset of the 1900s) as homes in general became increasingly larger. Various architectural plan books published during the 1840s and 1850s differentiated between cottages and villas or mansions, a distinction based on size and whether or not outbuildings, such as a carriage house or gatehouse, were included. With the 1842 publication of *Cottage Residences* by Andrew Jackson Downing, the North American public could suddenly select a home design to meet specific needs and budget requirements. The smaller cottages—romantic homes displaying all the charms of the medieval-inspired Gothic Revival style—came complete with arched windows and a restrained use of gingerbread trim that gave them an appealing signature look.

Henry Hudson Holly, architect and author of *Holly's Country Seats* (1863), expanded views on cottage building by pointing out that North American cottage architecture had a strong need for distinctive features and should not simply replicate English design. He made mention that

The owners of this small but picturesque Victorian cottage have chosen to accentuate its architectural details by painting the trim in shades of deep pink and lavender. The colors are echoed in the flowers that bloom in the cottage's front garden.

verandas were a necessity, as they were used to protect the house from the elements and to provide a spot for cool respite in the warm months. Holly also went to great lengths to stress his belief that a cottage should be built in an idyllic setting that complemented a simple architectural design rather than being "loaded down with unmeaning and expensive decorations." He felt that the architect should "combine beauty with the strictest utility," and he tried to do so in one of his own plans, known as "A Cheap Little Cottage." This particular design included a veranda, sitting room, and dining room (with a built-in china closet) on the first floor and three bedrooms and a linen closet on the second floor. The kitchen was located in the basement (a common arrangement in that era), and food was transported to the dining room via a dumbwaiter. Exterior decorations were kept to a minimum, though the plan did include distinct Italianate styling and resembled one of Holly's country villas. Holly strongly urged people to experience the benefits of life in the country, and his various plans, which were intended for country locations, promoted that practice.

The Victorian cottages designed for the working class during the mid-nineteenth century were larger than the cottage-type dwellings built in North America two hundred years earlier, but they were also quite small compared to those constructed between 1890 and 1910. Cities were becoming crowded, noisy, and polluted, so the well-to-do adopted the practice of summering at resorts located by the ocean, in the mountains, or near a lake. Owners of large hotels took to building small cottages on their properties to meet the ever-increasing demand. These cottage colonies became very much in vogue, thanks to the social status and privacy they afforded.

It was only a matter of time before wealthy industrialists began to build their own vacation homes, which were often quite massive in size. These grand summer mansions were also referred to as cottages or camps. While some of these homes were built of stone and even resembled châteaus, others were designed in a rustic style, Shingle style, or Queen Anne style. During this time, the cottage increasingly came to be viewed as a vacation home rather than as domestic architecture for the working class. Cottages, cabins, and chalets, ranging from small and cheerful to lavish and grand, sprang up at lake- and seaside locales, and picturesque towns were established in a variety of scenic locations all across Canada and the United States. Many of these resort towns remain popular today, and visitors to such diverse spots as Newport, Rhode Island; Martha's Vineyard, Massachusetts; Lake of the Woods, Minnesota; the Muskoka Lakes, Ontario; Cape Breton, Nova Scotia; and the many islands of the Pacific Northwest can experience the local historical cottage flavor.

While cottage architecture underwent a range of transformations throughout the early twentieth century, the appeal of a cozy, comforting refuge was—and is—so strong that we've never truly lost sight of its essence. Whether a weekend retreat, a summer getaway, a vacation destination, or a year-round home, today's cottage is a haven for rejuvenation, communing with nature, spending time with family and friends, or simply slowing down the pace.

Cottage decor calls for personal touches, and the cottage is the perfect place to display a collection that has been lovingly assembled over the years. In this cheerful kitchen, open shelves show off a collection of colorful pottery and dishware.

Cottage Living Today

There are several elements that evoke the architectural or decorative spirit of cottage style in its current interpretations. Although cottages are usually used as a vacation homes and are generally modest in size, they need not lack modern conveniences or amenities. The average cottage probably boasts between 1,000 and 2,000 square feet (93 and 186 sq m) of living space. Of course, some examples may be smaller, and some, in the tradition of the Victorians, may be grander.

Cottages generally boast an abundance of windows to take advantage of pleasing views and natural light, as well as a porch or deck to provide an outdoor living space. The facade is often dressed with a natural material—such as stone, shingles, clapboard, board-and-batten siding, logs, stucco, or brick—that relates to its location. If new, the cottage might not follow the dictates of a specific architectural style; instead, it might simply emulate the spirit of the cottage by making the most of the surroundings, integrating the setting into the design, and presenting a welcoming demeanor. On the other hand, it could just as well reflect an archetypal cottage design. In some instances, a cottage is fashioned from an existing structure, such as the rural farmhouse renovated as a country getaway or the boathouse transformed into an intimate seaside escape. One thing that all interpretations have in common is a thoughtful and efficient use of space.

The cottage interior is a highly personal space that offers a casual atmosphere while meeting practical needs. Built-ins such as window seats, bookcases, bunk beds, and china cupboards proliferate, thanks to their ability to make the best possible use of space. Low ceilings are another common trait, initially used for their energy-efficient property but often retained for their sense of intimacy. In contrast, a modern interpretation of the cottage may have a vaulted ceiling to create a sense of drama. Personal taste counts above all in the cottage, whether it serves as a seasonal retreat or a permanent home. After all, these structures are where we go for relaxation and revitalization—so they should cater to our individual tastes, personalities, and desires.

Decorating Your Cottage

Cottage decor is a free spirit. There are no rules, but there is an underlying sense of playfulness. The one constant is ambience. Since the main objective is relaxation, you should outfit rooms to be welcoming, comforting, and casual enough that you can kick off your shoes, curl up on the slip-covered sofa, and devote time to simple pleasures and pursuits. Cottage decor can be informal with just a hint of elegance, or it can be completely casual and laid-back. Often, an air of romance pervades. The choice lies in your hands.

In the chapters that follow, beautiful photographs reveal the various interpretations of cottage living today, many of which, of course, take their cues from the past. First, we will explore the charm of coastal retreats. From cedar-shingle Cape Cods perched on the bluffs to quaint Gothic Revival cottages basking in island breezes, these dwellings by the sea make the most of their settings to enchant all who enter. Soft colors and windows showcasing breathtaking views erase the lines between the indoors and sand-swept dunes.

From the coast, we travel inland to discover the pleasures of lakeside living. The tranquility of a cottage overlooking a lake is rivaled only by the surrounding natural beauty. From board-and-batten versions to more modernistic retreats, these cottages welcome visitors with the promise of waterfront views and activities. Interiors can be dressed up with rich jewel tones or pared down with neutral hues that let furnishings, accessories, and the great outdoors claim center stage.

Next, we celebrate the beauty of the open countryside. An American farmhouse on a country road, a stone chaumière in Provence, a thatched-roof cottage in England—each offers its own particular brand of charm. Rooms may wear a crisp white to highlight country details, a dramatic blend of colors to reflect the sun-baked earth, or muted shades to envelop a room in heartening warmth. A rural cottage may be home to a furnishing or two passed from generation to generation, wonderful reproductions, or a medley of comfortable pieces that blend as though they were meant for one another. The essence is one of genuine hospitality and nurturing comfort.

We leave the spaciousness of flower-filled meadows and grassy hills to see what the woods and mountains have to offer. Retreats in these settings include Adirondack camps, log homes, Alpine chalets, and other rustic variations. Appropriate palettes are discussed along with decorating for solid comfort and personal expression.

This cottage looks right at home in its surroundings, thanks to cedar shingles and dark green trim. At the corner of the wraparound deck, a painted green wooden rocking chair provides an ideal spot for savoring soft breezes and the invigorating scent of pine.

We take a look at such elements as furnishings, lighting, window treatments, storage ideas, accents, and the collections no cottage can do without.

Last but far from least, we take a close look at outdoor living spaces in all types of settings. The spirit of any cottage or vacation retreat is inextricably linked to the outdoors, and what better way to savor the view, the sounds and scents, and the unsurpassed beauty than in an outdoor living space? Worthy of special attention are critical elements of cottages—screened rooms, porches, decks, and patios—that bring us one step closer to nature.

CHAPTER ONE

Seaside Escapes

WE ARE DRAWN TO THE SEA—TO THE MAJESTIC SPLENDOR and incredible power of ocean waters. The tides, pounding surf, sandy beaches, and ragged cliffs have long inspired artists and writers. What is it about gazing out to sea that hypnotizes us so and lures us back again and again? Perhaps it is the sheer size of the ocean that holds us in awe, giving us a new perspective on life; the seemingly endless expanse of blue somehow makes our cares seem trivial and allows our spirits to soar.

There is an energy about the sea. Standing amid the dunes, you can feel it seep into every fiber of your being. It's a rebirth of sorts to revel in saltwater breezes while soft waves lap the shore. It's no wonder a cottage by the sea is something so many of us yearn for.

Early Cottages by the Sea

The call of the ocean has sounded for years. Long before the concept of a vacation retreat near the sea took root, fishermen and whalers built sturdy homes along the eastern coastline of North America to be near their livelihood. These dwellings, constructed during the eighteenth century, exhibited an English architectural influence. Typically small in size, they usually took one of two forms: the Cape Cod cottage or the New England saltbox.

The Cape Cod cottage, aptly named for the region in which the style originated, is a single story or a story and a half in height. Conducive to being added on to, this type of home often started out small, as a "half-size" Cape, and expanded as the family grew or as some other need for space arose. A great many of the early Cape Cods were

built by ship carpenters, who had special considerations in mind. For example, the framing techniques they used allowed for the possibility that they might need to move the house—via a team of horses—to a new site as sands shifted and the landscape changed. From the exterior, the Cape Cod was a tribute to simplicity, with its gray weathered shingles, gable roof, and intentional lack of ornamentation. Interiors were designed to be highly space-efficient, often following the example of ship cabins. The fireplace was the focal point as well a necessity for heating the home and cooking.

The Colonial or New England saltbox homes built along the Atlantic coast during the eighteenth century also had a distinctive look. The most salient feature of the saltbox is the lean-to addition at the rear. The early saltboxes also had a dramatic sloping roof, a rectangular floor plan, and double-hung windows. Like the Cape Cod, they were sided with shingles that weathered to a silver-gray.

Both classic architectural designs remain steadfast. In waterfront communities, older homes and fishing shacks are renovated or refurbished for seasonal or year-round use. New structures often combine an innovative approach with the familiar traditional lines of regional architecture to pay tribute to the local flavor. Their simplicity allows them to serve as subtle, quiet backdrops to the natural landscape.

Regional variations abound. On Nantucket, the religious influence of the early Quaker settlers led to box-shaped homes with shingled exteriors and board-and-batten (vertical planks with subtly decorative wood strips) doors. Other dwellings on the island exhibit a combination of designs, such as Cape Cod styling with a saltbox lean-to tacked onto the back. An impressive number of these early homes remain on the island, which is awash with charming cottages that wear the signature gray Colonial facade. In addition, many such cottages are enclosed by white picket fences and sport window boxes to showcase colorful blooms.

All along the Atlantic seaboard, Victorian architecture influenced the design of cottages. On Martha's Vineyard, a late-nineteenth-century Methodist campground for religious revivals evolved from a small community of seasonal tents, and later canvas-topped wooden structures that eventually became known as Carpenter Gothic cottages. Today a cluster of these diminutive cottages remains on the picturesque island, complete with colorful board-and-batten facades, gingerbread-trimmed front porches, and the hallmark double doors reminiscent of tent flaps. The typical romantic Carpenter Gothic on Martha's Vineyard stands a story and a half and features a gable roof and rectangular design. These fairy tale–like cottages and their postage stamp–size lots foster strong community spirit and devotion to island life.

Victorian architecture is also prevalent in other resort areas, such as Cape May, New Jersey, and in Canada's Maritime provinces, where striking Italianate and Queen Anne cottages line the streets that hug the shores; the rocky cliffs of Maine, where the Victorian Shingle style has left its mark; and the barrier islands

Opposite: *Taking on a new life, this boathouse has been transformed from a utilitarian space into a charming coastal cottage. With shoreline properties at a premium, it makes perfect sense to renovate outbuildings for seasonal or year-round living. The cupola atop this cottage pays tribute to the Victorian past and provides a prime spot from which to savor the view.*

Left: *A rainbow of Carpenter Gothic–style cottages line a shaded street in Maine. Throughout coastal New England, these Victorian-era treasures delight residents and visitors alike. Noted for their striking architectural details, these charming dwellings are bedecked with fanciful trim and quaint porches that foster community spirit.*

Bottom Left: *A shingled coastal cottage incorporates large picture windows that open up the small interior. Providing outdoor pleasure, a sturdy deck, complete with jaunty director's chairs, gives children a safe place to play until it's time for a swim.*

On the Florida coast, native foliage and tall grasses surround a pastel-painted cottage. A second-story porch allows residents to enjoy the view without having to disturb the natural plant life. Porches boast the added advantage of helping to keep interiors cool, a definite bonus in the South. The crowning feature of this inviting retreat is an intimate widow's walk, which provides an unencumbered 360 degree view.

off the coast of North Carolina. Large Shingle-style homes often combine the understated beauty of a shingled exterior with commanding stonework, which appears in the massive front porch.

Partly because of their more moderate climates, the southern Atlantic coast and the West Coast generally feature different types of architecture than the more northerly areas. Early Spanish settlers brought with them a building style that lives in harmony with the golden sunshine and the sun-kissed earth. Their early stucco ranch houses inspired Spanish Colonial Revival architecture during the first four decades of the twentieth century. Throughout Florida, Texas, and California, coastal vacation homes made of stucco with red tile roofs and decorative ironwork complement the seaside landscape. However, Victorian cottages dot the Pacific Northwest and resort areas along California's Pacific Coast Highway up into British Columbia.

Seaside Exteriors

It's almost guaranteed that if you have a cottage by the water, you'll be spending a great deal of time outdoors. Nonetheless, once inside, you'll still want to be able to gaze upon the sparkling sea that drew you to this special place to begin with. Thus, as with other types of cottages, windows are an important feature.

Double-hungs go hand in hand with Cape Cods, New England saltboxes, and Victorian architectural designs, but modern structures often employ several window types in order to serve a multitude of purposes. The site naturally influences window design, which will

On the rocky coast of Maine, a stone cottage appears to rise up out of the rugged landscape. Barn-board window shutters and Adirondack chairs on the deck have been allowed to weather to a silver-gray, thereby enhancing the natural appeal of this seasonal home.

ideally not only make the most of views but offer the opportunity to savor cooling coastal breezes. Plus, it is optimal to have plenty of access to the outdoors. Double or triple sets of French doors can line a living room wall to provide a smooth, easy transition to a full-length deck or porch. In another setting, a wall of casement windows might look out over a rocky cliff. Then again, the architectural beauty of a Palladian window may be used to frame a spectacular view.

When it comes to facades, special care is taken in selecting siding. While aesthetics are an important consideration, so too are more practical concerns. Natural elements can wreak havoc on a cottage's exterior, which needs to hold its own against saltwater sprays, strong winds, damp fogs, and the rays of the sun. There are a handful of products available that wear well and offer a wide range of decorative or simple but elegant looks.

Cedar clapboards, which can be painted or allowed to weather to a silver-gray, are appropriate for seaside cottages, as they establish a traditional look. Victorian and, occasionally, Cape Cod designs are good candidates for clapboard, which will last for many, many years. Industry experts recommend that clapboard be treated

with a primer on the front and back before paint is applied.

Vinyl siding with a wood grain pattern to give the appearance of clapboard is yet another option for seaside cottages, and some manufacturers offer a heavy-duty vinyl with locking pieces to withstand strong winds. Vinyl siding is available in different colors and with trim pieces appropriate to various architectural designs.

The cedar shingles used for exterior siding on seaside homes are typically either white cedar or western red cedar. In most cases, shingles, once applied, are allowed to weather to the beloved silver-gray. Investing in the best grade of shingles helps eliminate such problems as shrinkage or cracking.

A fairly new product, and one of special interest to owners of seaside homes, is fiber cement. Available in either shingle or clapboard form, fiber cement is rot- and wind-resistant. Furthermore, its composition won't alter with weather changes. This material does, however, require painting, which seems a small price to pay for the durability it provides.

Opposite: *A modern interpretation of the New England seaside escape combines cutting-edge architectural design with such traditional hallmarks as double-hung windows and cedar shingles. By incorporating a wraparound porch, the owner has gained a spacious outdoor living area that takes full advantage of sea breezes and breathtaking views.*
Above: *This quintessential Cape Cod cottage wears the signature gray that comes from allowing cedar shingles or clapboard to weather naturally. With no other homes in sight, the getaway affords privacy as well as fabulous vistas of the sea.*

Seaside Interiors

The interior of a seaside cottage evokes a feeling of serenity and a sense that, for the moment, time is standing still. Seaside interiors can be as diverse as their locales, often paying homage to a long and distinguished past or celebrating ties to the sea or the unspeakable beauty of the landscape.

The palette for a seaside cottage tends to be light and airy, following the lead of clear skies, tall grasses, and the subtle tints of beach pebbles and sand. White and other neutral hues create a quiet backdrop for spellbinding views, while blue contributes a calming quality reminiscent of the sea. Indeed, the combination of blue and white has long been favored for seaside cottages. But it is not the only successful palette. Pastels and other soft tints can form the basis for captivating seaside rooms, while muted shades with an aged look will complement a rustic wood-toned space or a more refined interior inspired by old sailing ships or Colonial architectural designs.

Walls are often composed of wood paneling, which can appear in many different forms, all of which contribute rich texture. Those interiors designed to recall the elegance of a luxury yacht or sailboat may have walls of amber-colored pine planks. Other seaside homes feature plank or beadboard walls painted a crisp white, which keeps the interior looking bright and cheery. Light blue and soft green paint also achieve successful results, tying the interior to the outdoor scenery. Either of the latter cool hues works especially well in a bedroom where you can enjoy gazing upon the stars and moon and drift into a peaceful sleep, lulled by the rhythmic sound of ocean waves.

Additional wall treatments include plaster color-washed in a beautiful ocher for a Spanish Colonial Revival cottage and tone-on-tone wallpaper in a neutral hue or a pale blue. Wallpaper comes in a host of fitting patterns, including shell designs, nautical themes, nature motifs, and romantic mini prints, and it is an effective means of establishing a dressier look. And don't forget about tile. Used for a fireplace surround, flooring, or even stair risers, colorful tiles contribute a stylistic flair

Above: *Life at a seaside cottage often involves paring down interiors to achieve simplicity. Here, occupants wake to a glorious view, so there's no need for fussy ornamentation. Pale lemon walls, wood flooring left bare, and windows dressed in crisp mini blinds form a low-key backdrop for just the essentials in furnishings. Small bursts of color are introduced by the pink and white quilt on the bed and a lovely collection of blue glass jars.*

Right: *A constant reminder of the ocean, a blue and white color scheme pervades this peaceful bedroom. Note how the various checkered and striped patterns mingle smoothly with the blue and white floral print adorning the chair cushion and the accent pillows on the bed. White walls, a white iron bed, and a Victorian wicker loop rocker help reinforce the breezy feel of this special retreat.*

Above: *In this upbeat living room, plank flooring has been painted a striking shade of blue. The space flaunts a playful spirit, thanks to the bold use of color and a smattering of star accents.*

Right: *Inspired by the beauty of a luxury sailing vessel, this seaside escape combines crisp, white plank walls with rich hardwood flooring and elegant wood trim on a space-saving spiral staircase. An open-living floor plan with a galley-style kitchen, loft bedroom, and abundance of windows makes the diminutive cottage seem larger.*

that's in keeping with Mediterranean style, Spanish Colonial Revival style, and more modern homes that rely upon natural color and texture. Hand-decorated tiles, especially ones with seaside or nautical designs, can have a particularly strong effect.

With sandy feet trekking in and out, flooring needs to be hardworking and easy to care for. Wood flooring has long been favored for its handsome good looks and natural texture. Aged pine boards wear a mellow patina that warms a casual room, but pickled or painted wood floors can also contribute relaxed airs. Deck enamel in gray, white, or blue can be used on floors along with a few coats of polyurethane to protect the finish. Hard floors can be softened with room-size sisal matting or other natural-fiber, needlepoint, or rag rugs.

Depending upon the size, age, and architectural design of a seaside getaway, the floor plan may include a traditional cottagelike series of rooms for different activities, or it may present an open-living design that allows areas to flow together. Regardless of a cottage's specific layout, though, space will almost certainly be at

This open-living floor plan keeps the cook in contact with family and guests. While both the kitchen and dining area are white, each is distinguished from the other by architectural embellishments. Kitchen windows play up the vaulted ceiling, and a long breakfast bar outfitted with stools draws the line between the cooking and dining areas.

a premium. As a result, owners have gotten pretty savvy when it comes to making the most of the square footage they have. One simple trick is to mine the nook underneath the stairs. Use decorative lattice panels in keeping with an airy decor or a small, latched door for easy access. In a living room where windows occupy much of the wall space, incorporate furnishings that don't obstruct the view or flow of traffic. A built-in banquette accessorized with plump cushions can easily fit beneath a bank of picture windows and offer plenty of seating without devouring valuable floor space. Plus, a resting spot such as this is great for stretching out your legs and soaking in the view. If the

banquette is designed with a hinged lid, you've got an extra spot for stashing clothes or games.

A kitchen that overlooks the living area is great for a cottage that hosts family gatherings or entertains guests. Since a cottage often serves as a place in which to reconnect and spend quality time with family, the lack of separation between these two main areas is ideal, promoting the sought-after togetherness. That's not to say that the spaces can't have a sense of definition. For example, a counter can serve as a room divider while providing storage and serving as a breakfast bar to boot. A large island, appropriately outfitted with stools or bar chairs, can function in much the

same way. Regardless of the layout, kitchens tend to be kept light and airy, with white or light wood cabinetry or open shelves. The bath can take its cue from the kitchen, incorporating a white or pale wood vanity to play up a natural color scheme or offer color contrast to deeper shades.

Family gatherings, weekend visitors, and special celebrations all mean plenty of houseguests. What to do if a cottage is short on bedrooms and there's no tiny guest house tucked away on the property? A screened porch can always be used as a sleeping porch, but don't forget to take your guests' privacy needs into consideration. The tent platform—basically a tent with a wooden

floor—used in nineteenth-century religious camps and in early mountain hunting camps has been updated with a crisp new look to offer overnight guests all the comforts of home. The contemporary version entails using a canopy made of weather-resistant fabric in tandem with a formerly open-air deck to fashion a cozy retreat. Add luxurious bedding, candles, or kerosene lamps and you've created a special and somewhat magical hideaway imbued with a hint of adventure. Of course, double-duty furniture can also be called upon to accommodate guests. Sleeper sofas are an easy solution, providing seating by day and a place to lay one's head at night.

An open floor plan allows everyone to do their own thing, yet still remain together. An abundance of natural textures—apparent in the wicker furnishings, wood-paneled walls, and assorted baskets filled with dried flowers—contributes to the appeal of this space.

Left: *Proving that simplicity can be both inviting and elegant, the interior of this cottage by the sea combines a neutral backdrop with white slip-covered seating and a handsome wood table. The open floor plan allows those in the dining area to share the view provided by windows in the living area. Left bare, these windows invite the landscape indoors, where nothing competes with the splendor of the natural surroundings.*

Above: *Half-moon windows lend charm to this cozy sleeping porch. During the day, French doors allow additional light to filter in, while at night, rod-hung curtains can be drawn closed to create a private retreat. A small sailing ship reminds guests of the seaside pursuits that await them after a good night's sleep.*

Sleeping arrangements and storage aren't the only practical concerns to address, though. Depending upon the region, you may experience a change of seasons, which means cool mornings and evenings as summer draws to a close. A fireplace built of brick (which can be beautiful when painted white) or stone, or with a wood surround and mantel, can take the chill off autumn days. Wood-burning stoves serve the same purpose and can be highly decorative given the wide range of colors and styles available. While some seaside cottages may depend upon ocean breezes for cooling, ceiling fans used throughout the house and even on the porch add extra comfort.

Furnishing Your Seaside Escape

When it comes to furnishing a seaside cottage, it's important to balance comfort, carefree appeal, and casual elegance. After all, when we escape to a seaside cottage, we want to stay put. As a result, entertaining is often done at home rather than at a club or restaurant. We revel in our private sanctuaries and want

others to be touched by their magic, too. But can a seaside retreat really be both sophisticated and casual? Absolutely.

Start with furnishings that echo the light and airy qualities of room backdrops. Natural textures are an excellent place to begin, so consider wicker and warm wood pieces. Wicker furnishings have graced the porches and interiors of cottages for well over a century. Styles range from Victorian and resort (some designs from the early 1900s were known as Bar Harbor, which boasted a latticework design, and Cape Cod, which consisted of tightly woven fibers) to Art Deco. Initially imported from England, assorted wicker furnishings were being made in Canada and the United States by the 1850s. Today, manufacturers are producing lines of wicker furniture for use indoors as well as pieces treated for outdoor use.

When purchasing wicker, check the chairs, rockers, tables, and settees for sturdy construction. Look for pieces with hardwood frames and nails rather than staples, which point to lesser-quality reproductions. Old wicker with a natural finish (sans paint) is a real find, since most antique wicker has been painted somewhere along the way. Paint, however, is no problem since white, brown, and even blue, green, or red wicker can be a wonderful addition to a seaside cottage.

Outfit wicker chairs with comfortable cushions, and feel free to use them in the living room, around the dining room table, or in bedrooms. Assorted wicker tables come in handy for stacking magazines and board games, showcasing a lovely vignette of shells or beach pebbles, or holding a bedside lamp and clock. And don't forget the wicker planter, which can be filled with flowers and set in a sunny window to create instant cheer.

Wood furnishings are available in a wide range of color tones. Pale or bleached woods complement a modern approach and harmonize quite nicely with a neutral or blue and white color scheme. Darker woods will contribute a rich look, often evoking old-world ambience or Colonial charm. Painted wood furniture is especially suited to a cottage decor with a country flair. Picture a chest of drawers with a painted seaside scene against a backdrop of fresh-looking white walls. Or how about a

Left: *Cottage bedrooms are no longer simply spaces for sleeping. They are also quiet havens where we can escape to read, relax, or ponder the scene out the window. Here, a painted white iron bed teams up with a white wicker night-stand (complete with draw-ers for keeping accessories close at hand) and a cozy wicker rocker. The latter has been painted a soothing shade of green that pro-vides a splash of color yet maintains the serene feel of the setting. A small vase of fresh flowers celebrates the beauty of simple pleasures.*

green painted blanket chest at the foot of an old iron bed, with a jaunty hooked rug nearby? Old benches and wooden trunks can be given an updated look with paint and go on to serve a multitude of functions around the beach house. In the kitchen or bath, white painted cabinets always look bright and fresh. Even something as simple as a painted hutch laden with dishware speaks volumes about a casual approach to seaside living.

Metal is another material often found in the decor of a seaside retreat. When you think of metal furniture in this setting, probably what comes to mind is the

Right: *At the foot of the bed, a painted chest pro-vides ample storage for clothing or blankets. With the addition of colorful pil-lows, it also becomes a make-shift window seat where you can wish upon a star or watch the sun rise.*

Above: *A blue-and-white color scheme unites the elements of this casual living room.*

Opposite: *This comfortable, relaxing living area features a primarily neutral palette that allows the marina view to take center stage. A jaunty blue and white striped easy chair adds a splash of color.*

image of iron or brass beds. Casual yet elegant, metal actually presents countless options way beyond the bedroom. Consider metal and wicker dining room chairs, metal and glass coffee tables or occasional tables, or a metal baker's rack to hold books, games, or kitchenware. Metal bar stools with attractive fabric seats host easy meals at a kitchen island. If you haven't explored the world of metal furnishings recently, you'll no doubt be surprised at the variety of finishes and decorative designs.

When it comes to furnishings, bringing the outdoors in is another popular theme. Pieces that are typically thought of in terms of outdoor spaces—such as

decks, porches, and patios—are surprisingly adaptable to cottage interiors. The director's chair, for example, with its simple wooden frame and colorful canvas seat and backing can be used instead of the traditional bar chair at a kitchen counter for relaxed dining. A wooden Adirondack chair accessorized with plump cushions is perfect for a quiet corner, and an English garden bench can make an entryway or mudroom more hospitable by offering a spot to sit down and remove wet or sandy footwear.

No seaside cottage is complete without an inviting sofa and plenty of easy chairs that you can sink into

Below: *Simplicity is the secret to the appeal of this dining area, in which pure white walls form the backdrop and splashes of brilliant color add sparkle. The simple yet elegant lines of Shaker-style furniture are not overwhelmed by the introduction of playful color in the intense blue of the buffet and the vibrant hues of painted fruit and fresh flowers.*

Right: *An abundance of white set off by wood trim and details maximizes the light, airy feeling of this large cottage kitchen. The woven textures of the baskets and window blind add a country touch, and gleaming copper pots complete the picture.*

on lazy afternoons, free from the pressure of having to be anywhere at any particular time. A seemingly simple indulgence such as this can do worlds to refresh your spirits. Fabrics and patterns can be chosen to have a soft and subtle effect or a more dramatic impact.

Cozy island cottages—especially those that have been in the family for years or that have a strong architectural history—tend to dictate, to a point, decorative direction. For instance, sofas and chairs upholstered in silks, brocades, or damask and handsome dark wood furnishings may be called for. Older pieces can be given an entirely new, fresh look when reupholstered. It's important to remember that you needn't follow the letter of the style. A wing chair makes a notable decorative statement when covered with a cheery blue and white striped fabric, and a Victorian settee takes on new life when treated to a colorful floral chintz. Stylized stripes (a stripe pattern including a floral design), large and small florals, tone-on-tone stripes, pictorial fabrics, checks, and cotton print slipcovers all achieve pleasing results in a cottage by the sea.

In contrast, a beachfront cottage that has large rooms or an open floor plan calls for a certain measure of easy elegance. Use fabrics noted for their durability and low-maintenance character, such as canvas, sailcloth, ticking, twill, or ottoman. As mentioned earlier, blue and white is the quintessential seaside color scheme, and stripes are a hands-down favorite when it comes to pattern. There are, of course, other equally attractive options, including textured fabrics in white, cream, or beige. White ribbed cotton fabric (in upholstery weight) with a striped or waffle-weave design or a white matelassé cotton with a raised pattern can be lovely when used on sofas and roomy chairs. Such fabrics have the perfect measure of soft pattern and are ideal in a minimalist setting or with a monochromatic color scheme to supply visual interest. Striped and textured fabrics are versatile, too—they blend easily with light, dark, or painted wood furnishings and metal pieces. Try upholstery with a nature-inspired motif; shells, seahorses, or stars are but a few possibilities. A motif can be used in just one room or throughout the cottage to create a unified look.

Left: *A narrow daybed takes full advantage of the magnificent view at this cottage in Maine. When the natural setting offers incomparable beauty, cottage decorators do well to simplify interiors and let the outdoors work its magic.*
Above: *Simplicity, particularly in the details, is the key to creating tranquility in a cottage setting. A white-painted headboard on a bed dressed in white linens offers a soothing resting spot. A rustic bench serves as a nightstand, and an old-fashioned lamp evokes a sense of the past.*

In a seaside cottage that conveys a sense of history, window dressings tend to be a bit formal. Rich fabrics with floral or striped patterns make elegant floor-length drapes that can be topped with a matching valance or accessorized with fringe, tassels, or nautical ropes. While formal treatments are best suited for a living room or dining room, bedrooms, baths, and kitchens will benefit from casual and crisp white Priscilla curtains, tab curtains, or cotton print curtains that can be looped back.

When only a hint of a window dressing is desired, look to something sheer or made of lace. Cotton batiste or cotton chambray panels are made with a variety of embroidered or appliquéd designs. A simple white sheer with embroidered stars or shells will ensure privacy, filter light, and, as an added bonus, billow in the breeze. For those who want to imbue a room with a touch of romance, lace curtains will set the mood.

Naturally, windows with a scenic view should be left bare, but even a picture window or bank of French doors may call for something to filter or block light from a rising or setting sun. That's where fabric shades or vinyl blinds (which can be rolled up out of the way when not in use) come in handy. Fabric shades can be custom-made to coordinate with furnishings, and vinyl blinds are available in all sorts of colors. There are also natural-looking bamboo shades, which enhance a seaside setting with their neutral or earth-tone hues.

When deciding upon lighting, look to your interior design scheme for inspiration. A traditional room might call for candlestick lamps with patterned or white fabric shades, while a more modern setting can be enhanced with metal- or pottery-based lamps sporting white, parchment, or colored shades. There are also table lamps in nautical themes, such as those with custom-crafted bases that resemble a lighthouse or a sailing ship. Others have bases made from driftwood. Use a combination of floor lamps, tabletop lamps, and wall sconces to provide general, task, and low-level lighting, respectively. In the dining room, a wrought-iron or metal chandelier situated above the table can be used in tandem with candles. Be sure to have plenty of votives or kerosene lamps on hand for evenings spent on the porch.

Above: *Blue and white make for a classic color scheme, and one that is especially resonant in a cottage that overlooks the water, as the interior echoes nature's own palette.*
Opposite: *There's no end to the possible decorative uses of natural materials once you put your imagination to work. Here, a one-of-a-kind headboard has been fashioned from an old piece of driftwood that, at first glance, seems to recall a ship's hull.*

Perhaps the most important ingredient in the seaside decorative mix is you. Incorporate the colors you love to live with, the furniture that meets your idea of comfort, and the fabrics that you find beautiful will ultimately shape your vacation retreat. Let the blue sky and shimmering ocean inspire you.

Accessories and Collectibles

Decorating a cottage at the shore should be a pleasure-filled, spirit-lifting, and rewarding experience. A seaside escape is a special place associated with good times, relaxation, family and friends, in some cases nostalgia, and above all the enchanting beauty of nature. Once the mood of the cottage is set with the right color scheme and furnishings, it's time to focus on the details.

There's no question that wood and tile floors are beautiful, but sometimes we desire rugs for a bit of cushioning underfoot or a definition of space. Colorful hooked rugs with a nautical or seascape theme, braided rugs, vibrant dhurrie rugs, and rag rugs are ideal. Some hooked rugs are so beautiful that you may be tempted to use them as wall art rather than placing them on the floor. During the second half of the nineteenth century, the eastern seaboard of North America was a hotbed of hand-hooked rug activity. Women crafted rugs with geometric designs, floral motifs, animal illustrations, and even homey mottoes. Early examples made by the wives of seafaring men often featured seashells, fish, or anchors, and while these vintage treasures are more likely to turn up in

museums than in antiques shops, the art has most definitely been revived. Coastal shops often carry hand-hooked rugs crafted by talented artisans, and you can also purchase kits should you prefer to craft your own family heirloom.

Some of the best decorative objects are found on morning strolls along the beach or hikes around the rocky shore. Children love collecting shells and will be eager to join in the hunt. Fill a platter with shells and display it on the coffee table, or line pieces along a mantel. Or gather some colorful sea glass into a clear bowl for a lovely yet understated centerpiece. You could also put your creative genius to work and make a shell-studded picture frame, wreath, or keepsake box. Collect shells, pieces of driftwood, and beach pebbles in a wire basket, rinse them off while still in the basket, allow to dry, and voilà—you've got the perfect accent for that end table by the couch.

A seaside cottage can never have enough baskets. The Nantucket lightship basket, composed of tightly woven cane, was made along the New England coast during the nineteenth century. While antique versions may be hard to find, talented artisans, many located on the island of Nantucket, are turning out exquisite reproductions in many different sizes. Other baskets crafted in coastal regions are made of reed or sea grass. Their simplicity, texture, and coloring give them enduring charm. Try hanging a few from the ceiling beams for an eye-catching diversion overhead; doing so will also make a room feel more cozy.

Whether vintage or brand-new, baskets can do double duty as storage containers, taming clutter and rounding up necessities we like to keep close at hand. Use baskets in the kitchen to hold utensils or linens, in the bath to hold soaps and toiletries, in the living room for magazines and logs, or on the porch for games and flowers.

In just about every coastal area, you'll find a treasure trove of antiques shops, art galleries, and specialty stores. Visit a variety of these to find that perfect seascape or old print of a clipper ship to hang above the mantel. While you're at it, don't forget to track down a warm wool throw and plenty of decorative pillows to

Left: *An old wooden sign perched atop a long bench holds pride of place in this vibrant setting. How could the owners resist such a find when the room's color-washed walls clearly reflect one of the rich hues that appear in the sky at the end of the day? Casual rattan furnishings enhance the tropical mood of the space, while brightly hued ceramic pots hold magazines.*
Below: *Even a small cottage bath can be big on style. With a blue and white color scheme reminiscent of the sea, this cozy bath calls upon favorite paintings and blue and white accessories to give it a personal touch.*

toss onto the sofa. Extra quilts come in handy in the bedrooms, and for a fanciful touch, soft netting draped around the bed can form a canopy reminiscent of a tropical setting.

Old maps and navigational charts, wood-carved duck decoys, carved ivory, boat models, buoys, and even ship life preservers make splendid additions in a cottage by the sea. Consider, too, collectibles not necessarily related to the ocean but that display colors reminiscent of the beach. For example, old blue glass bottles or jars can hold flowers on the mantel or on a window ledge. Another possibility is pottery in soft or muted shades of blue and green that look right at home at the shore. Look for vases and bowls, and fill them with flowers or fruit—or display the pieces in a grouping where the beauty of the pottery speaks for itself.

CHAPTER TWO

Lakeside Cottages

> Lo! The level lake
> And the long glories of the winter moon.
>
> —Alfred, Lord Tennyson,
> *The Lady of Shalott*, 1832

There is something about the serene beauty of a lake that captivates us. Its presence evokes childhood memories of searching for just the right stone to skip across the water's glassy surface and of swimming in invigorating waters surrounded by nature. Enjoying a picnic luncheon on the dock in the summertime and skating across a frozen pond on a starry winter's night are pieces of the past that call us home as adults. Knowing full well the pleasures that await us in a lakeside retreat, we journey to these areas for respite from the workday world.

Lakeside Cottages of Yesteryear

There is no one architectural style when it comes to lakeside living. Rather, particular styles or uses of materials may have taken hold in certain regions. In years past, lakeside homes, especially those built by fishermen and hunters, were more rustic than refined.

Vacation retreats were last on the list of priorities for many during the 1930s and 1940s, but after World War II, the housing boom that led the masses to suburbia also fostered a growing trend toward family vacations. The middle class of the 1950s and 1960s vacationed in board-and-batten or clapboard-covered cottages on the shores of lakes to enjoy family time together and experience a respite from the routine. Swimming, boating, and picnicking outdoors were the order of the day. So beloved were these lakeside escapes that they were often passed down from one generation to the next, each leaving its mark with small changes and improvements.

With ambitious land development, better roads, and favorable economic periods, remote or rural lakes became easily accessible. By the 1980s, small vacation homes were being built at a rapid pace. Older cottages on rivers and

lakes were modernized, expanded, or torn down to make way for more luxurious accommodations with captivating views. Lakeside living is often associated with shingled or clapboard cottages in the east, while log cabins dot the lake shores in the Midwest and Pacific Northwest. Victorian cottages and plantation-style homes have proved popular in the southern states, and modern architecture has led to some truly innovative designs in California. But the one thing these dwellings all have in common is that familiar, informal cottage-style air.

Lakeside Exteriors

The well-designed lakeside cottage is often constructed with more than summer vacations in mind. We are thinking about the future, planning such homes to serve as year-round retreats where we can savor the setting during the change of seasons. Many lakeside cottages are also planned as residences in which to enjoy retirement years.

When it comes to size, efficiency, and use of space, zoning restrictions and building regulations vary from one area to the next, but the trend is toward smaller homes that are low-maintenance, energy-efficient, and graced by an abundance of outdoor living space. There is also a trend toward doing it ourselves. Instructional books and building plans for simple, small cottages

Page 45: *Relaxing comes easy in a lakeside cottage with rustic airs. A stone backdrop recalls the outdoor surroundings, while a plump sofa and armchair speak of indoor comfort. All seating is accessorized with toss pillows for curling up before the fire. The clever use of a wood shelf along the wall creates out-of-the-way space for collectibles.*

Left: *With a facade of cedar shingles and dark green trim, this lakeside getaway blends effortlessly with the environment. The location, a mere strip of land with water surrounding it, affords scenic vistas from every angle.*

Below: *A screened-in porch is a cottage delight, offering the pleasures of the outdoors without the extremes of weather or the distraction of pests.*

allow someone with a desire to build his or her own vacation home the opportunity to accomplish much of the project. For those who prefer to work with an architect or builder, talented professionals can make lifelong dreams come true.

Whether building from scratch or renovating an existing lakeside cottage, siting is an important factor. Being sensitive to the natural landscape often calls for innovative designs that work around trees and accommodate slopes or rocky terrain. Windows play a major role in the appearance and pleasure of a lakeside home and afford endless opportunities for bringing

the outdoors inside. Double-hung, casement, and sliding windows are used on traditional designs, along with large picture windows and French doors. Small or large windows with angled, half-moon, or Palladian designs can be used in contemporary cottages for a signature touch. Skylights can open up an under-the-eaves bedroom and introduce an abundance of natural light while permitting continued enjoyment of the blue sky above from within the cottage.

In some cases, a lakeside cottage's grounds may include a boathouse with an upper story or attic hideaway that can be transformed into guest quarters. The area below can function as storage space for any over-flow from the cottage as well as for boating gear. Often looking like a miniature replica of the main cottage, the boathouse can incorporate the same window designs and exterior siding as its companion. In many cases, boathouses are converted to function as full-fledged cottages. Saying goodbye to their initial function, these structures become cozy and congenial dwellings.

When it comes to the exteriors of lakeside homes, building materials are chosen with longevity, sensitivity to the environment, and easy maintenance in mind. Cedar clapboard and shingles, which weather to a soft brown-gray, are popular siding options. Combine clapboard or shingles with dark green trim, and the lakeside home will blend harmoniously with the natural surroundings. Or paint the whole exterior; the facades of many lakeside cottages are dressed in dark green, brown, or deep red.

Vinyl siding is another material that appeals to a great many lakeside homeowners because it is virtually maintenance-free (wash it yearly to keep it looking its best). It's also easily adapted to several architectural styles. Victorian-style cottages and modern dwellings often make use of vinyl siding, which is available in a wide range of colors and assorted trim pieces.

Lakeside Interiors

The interior space of a lakeside home should meet personal and/or family needs. While cottages traditionally consist of a series of small rooms, some owners may opt for a roomy, open-living floor plan. There's always the possibility of compromise or having the best of both worlds. A small lakeside cottage can be made to appear more spacious by opening up the living area, dining area, and kitchen to create a great room and by incorporating a bank of windows to invite the water-front view. While public spaces encourage group activities and family interaction, intimately sized bedrooms offer individual, private sanctuaries.

Since many lakeside cottages are built without a basement as a cost-effective measure, creating storage space entails thinking in new ways. A mudroom off the

kitchen will give you an organized area for sports or boating equipment and gear, but storage needs don't stop there. Built-in shelves for books and collectibles, window seats with lift-up lids or drawers, built-in dressers, and bunk beds are all cottage favorites, as appropriate to a lakeside retreat as to a rustic woodland cottage. The kitchen, too, can be viewed with a critical eye when it comes to storage. Purchasing smaller appliances will free up cupboard space. An under-the-counter refrigerator and a narrow stove will open up a great deal of wall space, which can be devoted to a pantry cupboard. In addition, kitchen cabinets that go all the way to the ceiling rather than leaving a foot (30cm) or more of empty space will increase storage. The secret lies in assessing your needs carefully.

Perfectly situated and designed in harmony with its setting, this cottage features cedar shingles and locally quarried stone. The wraparound deck furnished with a pair of Adirondack chairs offers an unbeatable spot to simply sit and take in the lakefront scene.

Right: *This delightful screened porch has been designed to reflect its best-of-both-worlds setting. The wood finish links the space to the abutting woods, while white wicker furnishings and a lamp with decorative fish provide ties to the beach.*

Below: *A lovely stone hearth becomes the focal point in this serene living room. In addition, large windows throughout create dramatic impact tempered by a neutral color palette. Bouquets of fresh flowers and an oil painting atop the mantel add just a hint of garden color.*

The interior color scheme takes its cue from the lake environment. An intimate lakeside cottage in a heavily wooded area reflects a rustic charm by calling upon wood tones and nature-inspired hues. This is the cottage ideally suited to knotty-pine paneled walls or a combination of beadboard paneling and painted wallboard. A rustic feel can also be achieved by leaving walls uncovered to expose the framing or by using board-and-batten panels. For something a bit more elegant, panel a fireplace wall with a warm wood tone, such as honey pine, and paint the plasterboard walls throughout the rest of the living area in a neutral or nature-reflecting hue, such as khaki or moss. Jewel-tone colors also have merits in a lakeside setting. Not only do they contribute subtle richness to a carefree decorating style, but they also blend effortlessly with deeper wood tones. A tone-on-tone wallpaper or a wallpaper with a nature motif can also be introduced, adding color as well as decorative pattern. The stylized floral and nature designs of the Arts and Crafts Movement that are available in wallpaper today will fittingly enhance a lakeside cottage furnished with a mélange of rustic and Mission oak pieces. Wallpaper is often favored in bedrooms to infuse a smaller space with charm and personality.

For flooring, consider salvaged pine planks to provide that much-appreciated patina that comes with age. Hardwood flooring, usually appearing in the form of oak, is also popular. Wood laminate can be employed in bathrooms or kitchens, along with tile or resilient flooring. For mudrooms, use something that's easy to clean, such as tile or slate. Calling to mind a rocky lake shore, slate eases the transition between indoors and out.

Of course, not all lakeshore cottages are surrounded by dense woods; some are out in the open. Such cottages are often decorated to reflect the color of water and the endless sky. In this type of setting, a white backdrop is one appropriate way of conveying an informal and relaxed lifestyle. There are so many variations

Wood tones and walls left uncovered to expose rugged framing convey a relaxed cottage lifestyle. A slip-covered sofa, a cushioned easy chair, and a pine harvest table with painted chairs contribute creature comforts without putting on airs.

Below: *A red brick fireplace provides both physical and visual warmth in this living room, which features white board-and-batten walls and a vaulted wood-beamed ceiling. Slipcovered furnishings in blue and white contribute to the laid-back feel of the space.*

of white, though, that it can actually be difficult to make a final selection. Do you lean more toward ivory or prefer basic white? How about something with just a soft hint of blue? Study color chips carefully to find your perfect shade of white, and combine it with accents reflecting the glimmer of a blue lake, the green of a grassy landscape, or the cheery yellow of the midday sun. If a bit more color is desired, try pastels, which like white will open up a modest-size cottage and infuse the rooms with a whisper of springtime that will remain constant throughout the seasons.

Right: *Porch perfection: sliding doors and screens open this porch to the outdoors while protecting it from the elements, making nature accessible year-round. Simple furnishings include whitewashed chairs & a versatile table. A stone floor makes for easy upkeep.*

Year-round or even seasonal use of a lakeside cottage can call for a fireplace or wood-burning stove to take the chill out of the air. River or lake stones are often used for the fireplace itself or for a fireproof wall behind the stove. Brick or tile can also be employed to create a fireplace or safety wall, but be sure to check local rules and regulations. It's also wise to check the local laws and your insurance company regulations regarding the installation of a wood-burning stove. There are myriad options available when it comes to state-of-the-art stoves. Do you prefer to burn logs, or are you open to the possibility of a pellet stove? There

Lakeside Cottages

Opposite: *This lakeside*
cottage is big on theme
accessories. A wooden
canoe presides overhead,
drawing the eye up toward
the vaulted ceiling, and a
corner cabinet that repli-
cates a canoe houses the
television. Even a couple
of wooden oars get in on
the act by serving as
whimsical curtain rods.

are advantages and disadvantages to each, so it's worth exploring your choices carefully.

Furnishing the Lakeside Cottage

As with any cottage, furnishings for a lakeside home should cater to individual tastes. Comfort is paramount, as is a casual and carefree style. Since there are no hard and fast rules, there are endless opportunities for creating a highly personalized retreat.

Start by considering your location and developing a wish list of furniture items. A lakeside retreat in a wooded area may inspire a more rustic approach to outfitting rooms, while a cottage surrounded by nothing but open space may have a contemporary or romantic bent. Introduce rustic airs by including a singular object such as a twig table or a comfy hickory rocker. Mission-style, wicker, and twig furnishings have long been admired for their compatibility and are well suited to a mix-and-match approach.

Arts and Crafts– or Mission-style furniture became popular in North America during the early 1900s. Gustav Stickley, father of the American Arts and Crafts Movement, introduced a style of oak furnishings with clean, linear shapes; a dark, smoky finish; and pegged joints. Upholstered pieces were usually outfitted with leather, and any metalwork, such as hinges or drawer pulls, was made of copper or iron.

The beauty of the original Arts and Crafts furnishings lies in their simple design and honest workmanship. While signed antique pieces are rare and quite expensive, L. & J.G. Stickley, Inc. continues to produce authentic Stickley designs, and a number of noted specialty shops are currently turning out quality reproductions of vintage pieces. Similar furnishings can also be obtained through popular home fashion catalogs. Many of these latter pieces have been given an updated look with fabrics sporting botanical, plaid, or kilim patterns or tone-on-tone designs featuring leaf or other nature motifs.

Other furnishings that will find themselves at home in most lakeside abodes include painted chairs, cupboards, tables, benches, beds, chests, and trunks.

Several furniture manufacturers offer lines with a relaxed, "cottage" lifestyle in mind. If you prefer something with a little more history and character, turn to secondhand furnishings, which can quickly attain new life with a fresh coat of paint. "Theme" furnishings, such as an old canoe cut down and fitted with shelves to serve as a bookcase, are instant conversation pieces that inject a cottage with a sense of imagination. Scout large outdoor antiques shows for old iron beds, tables, chairs, and whatever else strikes your fancy. Inspiration is everywhere—in every quilt, table, chest, or plain white pitcher—so keep your eyes open for that special something.

Bright or deep blues, greens, reds, browns, and jewel tones are beautiful featured in plaid, floral, and tone-on-tone patterns for upholstery. Solid-color chairs and sofas upholstered in mohair will wear like iron and actually look luxurious when they feature a deep green or garnet red. And don't discount slipcovers: they allow you to change the look of your furnishings, and thus your overall décor, with the change of seasons or when the whim strikes. Always select fabrics for easy care and durability. After all, the cottage is a no-worries environment. Everyone should feel free to put their feet up while sipping iced tea or nibbling on a crumbly muffin.

For a more sophisticated or minimalist approach, blue and white striped fabrics (always a favorite in any home located near the water), tea-stained florals with a soft, aged look, and solid-color cotton corduroy fabrics blend easily with wicker, pale wood, or painted furnishings.

In kitchens and baths, cupboards and other cabinetry can take on various looks, from rustic to more formal. Knotty pine and beadboard cabinets will convey a rustic air, while cabinetry painted forest green adds a woodsy feeling. Bright white cabinetry, light wood maple cabinets, and even open metal shelves impart a modern and airy feeling. For something a little unexpected in the bath, consider converting a handsome chest of drawers or a vintage sideboard into a vanity, complete with a decorative china sink.

Opposite: This lakeside retreat is filled with color and cottage style, thanks to casual furnishings and theme accessories. Dark green shutters with pine tree cut-outs jazz up architectural wood posts, which draw an imaginary line between the dining area and living room, while a toss pillow featuring a majestic deer provides a fitting accent against the plaid upholstery of the sofa. In the center of the living area, a painted trunk takes on a new career as a coffee table.

Right: A close-up of the trunk reveals its various handpainted designs. Notice how the faded paint and gently worn edges impart a sense of times past that fits in with the casual mood of the space.

Accessories and Collectibles

You may have cosmetically attractive rooms and the most comfortable, inviting furnishings possible, but without select decorative accessories and collectibles on display, your lakeside home will lack that personal touch that transforms it into a true haven. The key word is select, or carefully chosen, accessories and collectibles that convey or pay tribute to a lakeside lifestyle and your interests. Pare decorative accessories down to avoid an interior that competes with lake views, and look to organized ways of displaying collections. As with any modest-size space, one of the best ways to accessorize a cottage is by incorporating accents that are not only pleasing to look at but functional as well. For example, a collection of ceramic pitchers can hold flowers and be used to serve refreshing drinks. Likewise, earthy stoneware jars can present an eye-catching display while keeping kitchen tools and various odds and ends conveniently out of the way.

Plump pillows and warm wool or cable-knit throws on sofas and easy chairs are a necessity for cool evenings spent in front of the fireplace or wood-burning stove. Pillows can sport plaid, checkered, floral, Navajo, or nature prints—all of which are in keeping with a more traditional lakeside decor. Solid-color pillows in forest or Alpine green, chestnut, navy blue, cranberry, or beige will offer visual contrast on a sofa dressed in a print fabric. Then again, pillows made from vintage floral fabrics and finished with a colored braid or fringe may be better suited to the character of your home.

Area rugs offer an easy way of introducing vibrant or subdued color and pattern to cottage rooms while providing welcome cushioning underfoot. Choose rugs that are treated for stain resistance, and if you decide to go with wool, make sure it's mothproof. Hooked rugs can be purchased with nature motifs that complement a vacation home, while rag rugs typically feature jaunty stripes or colorful checks. Braided rugs can boast a rainbow of colors or feature one predominant hue, such as blue, green, or red. Bringing an oriental rug into a living area imbues the space with traditional airs and a

Above: *This lakeside cottage bedroom calls upon color and accessories to give it style and warmth. Soft green walls and hardwood flooring bring natural hues indoors, while a folk-art bench, red plaid pillows, and a patterned bedspread imbue the room with spirit. The fishing pole and framed fish print celebrate outdoor pursuits.*

Opposite: *Rustic charm fills every room in this log cabin by a lake. A colorful, striped throw serves as a decorative tablecloth, while a Native American rug featuring similar hues defines the dining space. Straw hats and old fishing signs call attention to lakeside activities.*

The children's bathroom
in this log cabin makes
cheerful use of red, white,
and blue details, while the
basic elements of the
room—walls and undersink
cabinet—are either white
or wood, making it a simple
matter to change the decor
as the children grow up.

A cottage bath can have all the amenities of a pampering spa, but if the lighting is too harsh, the sense of tranquillity is ruined. Here, fixtures mounted above the archway provide soft illumination, throwing light up to the white vaulted ceiling, which reflects it back down. Natural light enters at the window, where it is gently filtered by lacy panels that contribute old-fashioned charm. Other traditional touches include beadboard wainscoting, a pedestal sink, and a painted chest of drawers used to hold towels, soaps, and toiletries. And what better place for a calming bubble bath than a claw-foot tub housed in its own secluded alcove?

touch of timeless elegance. Striking machine-made examples, made in England or Belgium and exported to the United States, are ideal since they are often just as striking as handcrafted rugs but far less costly. Use rugs in the living room, hallways, bedrooms, and baths for warmth and visual interest.

Other textiles important to have on hand in a lakeside cottage are warm sheets and bedcoverings. Cotton sheets are fine for the summer months, but come autumn you'll want to have flannel bedding, wool or polyester fleece blankets, and goose-down comforters to snuggle under. Flannel sheets are made in a variety of colors, and wool blankets are available with colorful Native American prints or cheerful stripes. A mix of red and black stripes is one combination long favored in rustic retreats, as is a white background with green, yellow, red, or blue stripes. Polyester fleece, the new darling of cooler-climate living, is now used for blankets as well as clothing. Fleece blankets and throws come in all sorts of colors, making them easy to coordinate with any decor. And more importantly, they are surprisingly warm, durable, and easy to care for. During the colder months of the year, keep them draped over the seating in the living area for easy access. When it's warmer, they can be stashed in a blanket chest or window seat. An old-fashioned wooden trunk acting as a coffee table can be the perfect spot for stowing these coverings during the months in which they're not needed. Comforters, especially those made with goose down, are rated for cool temperatures. These and other bedding options are sold at fine home furnishings stores and through mail-order catalogs.

Lamps with vintage styling, such as the banker's lamp with a green glass shade, are fitting additions on a desktop or a bedside table. Arts and Crafts–inspired fixtures with copper trim and colored glass or mica shades also work well in a lakeside setting. Wrought-iron floor lamps, table lamps, and chandeliers are versatile enough to use with a rustic decor, in a more contemporary setting, or in a log cabin with a western theme. Select lampshades of basic white linen, print fabrics (florals or checks), or parchment. In kitchens, recessed lighting fixtures are efficient and unobtrusive,

Left: *This rustic bedroom is an homage to the outdoor life, with one-of-a-kind beds crafted from logs still covered in bark, plus assorted woodsy details including canoe paddles and a stuffed fish. The plaid pattern of the chair and curtains is wittily echoed in the ceiling fan, while denim bed coverings add another textural element.*

Above: *: A cozy guest bedroom strikes a serene yet stylish note with a few retro touches, including an old-fashioned coverlet and a vintage wicker chair that does double duty as a nightstand.*

ideal qualities in an area that typically holds lots of items in a small amount of space. The bath, on the other hand, usually calls for a ceiling fixture and wall sconces positioned on either side of the mirror.

When it comes to adorning a window that has a lakeside view, less is definitely more. Whenever possible, leave windows bare to take full advantage of the scenery outside. After all, part of the attraction of such a cottage is its offering of front-row seats to nature's show. Fabric or bamboo shades that roll up out of the way can be called into use when some sort of window treatment is needed for privacy or for blocking out light. When something dressy is desired, consider a floral, checkered, or striped valance. Simple tab or cotton print curtains will fill the need for window dressing in bedrooms, as will a valance used in tandem with a basic roller shade.

Above: *Favorite elements of country style—vintage quilts and linens, a rustic cupboard, and found objects including faded outdoor signs and a well-used paddle—transform this simple bedroom into a cozy cottage haven.*

Right: *A western theme is on tap in this lakeside cottage bath, thanks to a plethora of cacti, horseshoes, and various old iron implements. White walls and terra-cotta floor tiles make a fitting backdrop for the different accoutrements, while a sumptuous tub with a river-rock surround creates the impression of bathing in a lake.*

Opposite: *This lakeside log home boasts panoramic views courtesy of a soaring wall designed with large picture windows. Free of drapes or blinds, the expanses of glass put the breathtaking scenery on perpetual display. Thanks to the open floor plan, nature's show can be relished while dining at the table or relaxing in the living area. A round oriental rug contributes timeless elegance, while a beloved sailboat pays homage to the lakeside locale. Nestled into a formerly empty corner, a pair of oars makes a decorative statement.*

Shells, driftwood, river rocks, or lake stones can be used to design striking vignettes. They'll bring the spirit of the outdoors inside, serving as small reminders of the landscape around you. Gather them together on a tabletop, sprinkle them along a windowsill, or collect them into a basket in the bath. In general, baskets are always good to have on hand, as they can be put to work at a moment's notice to hold sundry goods. Such metal objects as galvanized pails and watering cans make endearing containers for flowers, fresh or dried.

Anything to do with fishing and boating is fair game for a lakeside cottage collection. Colorful lures, wicker creels (lidded baskets for fish), vintage fishing poles, canoe paddles, and even old canoes themselves make a devoted collector's heart beat just a little faster. Old lures can be grouped and framed to create wall art, creels can be hung on old iron hooks, and poles or paddles can be displayed above the mantel, over a doorway, or high up on the wall in a room with a vaulted ceiling. Framed black and white photos depicting lake scenes, fishermen in action, or lakeside cottages and resorts can be found at antiques shops specializing in rustic memorabilia.

What else do collectors hunt for when filling their lakeside cottages? Vintage quilts are certainly a big draw. With their bright colors and bold patterns, vintage quilts are perfect for bringing homespun charm to a cottage bedroom. And they're not just for the bed: drape one over the back of a plain wooden chair to give the simple furnishing some pizzazz, or rest one atop a trunk at the foot of the bed. You can even hang one on the wall just above the bed to create a festive headboard of sorts. While quilts from the nineteenth century are hard to come by and are thus rather expensive, ones made between 1920 and 1940 are still readily available.

Wood-carved decoys are other objects of desire. Antique handcrafted examples, often considered folk art, were made throughout the nineteenth century until the early 1900s, when factory-produced versions arrived on the scene. Early decoys—mainly ducks, geese, and shore birds—were carved by hunters and craftsmen up and down the eastern coastline as well as in the Great Lakes region. Handcrafted examples are ideal, but there's also a strong market for decoys produced at certain factories, such as the Mason Decoy Factory, which was in business in Detroit until the late 1920s. Antiques dealers specializing in rustic accessories and folk art are the best source for vintage decoys.

What else strikes your fancy? What motivates you to be up and out of bed at five in the morning to rush off to an antiques show or attend an auction? Perhaps it's the old pottery bowls you keep stacked in the kitchen and use for cooking. Maybe it's old postcards from the golden era of resort hotels. Could it be the old china collection you keep adding to for dinners at the cottage? No matter what you collect, remember that over the long term, buying the best example you can afford is the best investment. Quality, not quantity, is what counts when building a collection of cherished objects.

Left: *This kitchen takes on character with an artfully arranged display of fishing and boating gear hanging from the ceiling, as well as wood-carved ducks resting on a sunny window ledge.*

Above: *A rustic display niche becomes the perfect spot to showcase lake stones and a charming sailboat. Such souvenirs of walks along the shore and trips to local antiques shops may not cost a fortune, but the memories they recall are priceless.*

CHAPTER THREE

Rural Getaways

> May the countryside and the gliding
> valley streams content me.
>
> —Virgil

ROLLING HILLS, GREEN VALLEYS, WILDFLOWER MEADOWS, acres of fruit trees, sprawling vineyards, and land as far as the eye can see evoke images of the idyllic rural dwelling. Wide-open spaces offer respite from crowded cities, tight schedules, the sensory overload of our high-tech world, and the stress so often associated with the pressures of everyday life. As a weekend retreat, a seasonal vacation home, a permanent residence, or even a family-run business, the rural dwelling allows us to slow the pace, rediscover the natural beauty and bounty of the countryside, and immerse ourselves in a simplified lifestyle—the country lifestyle. This passion for country living is shared throughout the world. In France, England, and Ireland, for instance, old stone houses and thatched-roof cottages are being restored, and outbuildings are being reconfigured as living spaces. And in the United States and Canada, barns and carriage houses are being transformed into gracious cottage retreats.

The Earliest Country Houses

More than two hundred years ago, the vast majority of the population looked to farming for its livelihood. Farmhouses with barns, chicken coops, and assorted other outbuildings dotted the landscape in large numbers, often housing extended families that worked together for the common good. As times changed, urban areas grew and employment and educational opportunities expanded, drawing people away from the countryside to make a fresh start in towns and cities. In the process, farming was greatly abandoned as a life's calling. During recent years, however, we have been reversing our tracks and seeking refuge in greener pastures.

In the past twenty years or so, there has been a growing trend toward country living—both for everyday life and for vacations. The number of quaint country inns and romantic bed-and-breakfasts has skyrocketed. Many such

establishments are owned and operated by city folks that have traded the glamour, glitz, and high-paying, high-stress jobs of the city for what they consider a more fulfilling way of life. At the same time, vacationers originally content with just a few precious days in the country have begun to buy property there, either building their own dream cottages or renovating existing houses to meet their visions of the ultimate getaways. And these treasured dwellings are not just to be enjoyed in the summer months: autumn brings the beautiful color of the changing leaves on the trees; winter offers the serenity of a flat or rolling landscape blanketed in white: and spring, with its powers of rebirth, presents meadows filled to overflow with colorful blooms. Even in those areas with less distinctive seasons, the countryside never fails to delight and amaze us with subtle shifts in color and ever-changing beauty.

In different areas throughout the United States and Canada, farmhouses and country cottages display the building styles once popular in those regions. For example, stone or brick farmhouses were once built by both German and Dutch settlers throughout such mid-Atlantic states as Pennsylvania, New York, Maryland, and New Jersey. By the early eighteenth century, two-story stone or clapboard Georgian houses were constructed as plantation homes in the South or as village residences for prosperous merchants along the East Coast. Several decades later Federal-style homes were being built throughout the East and Midwest. Then the early 1800s saw many a rural cottage in the Great Lakes region constructed of cobblestone—lake stones worn smooth over time.

Many of the farmhouses built during the early nineteenth century were simplified versions of the Greek Revival style that swept the United States and Canada between the 1820s and 1860s. While many southern mansions from this period were grand examples of Greek Revival architecture that boasted large gabled porticos supported by massive Doric columns (often called a temple front), the Greek Revival farm-house was typically built with small columns featured as pilasters flanking the front door and a kitchen wing located off one side of the house. Various interpretations of the style appeared across the continent.

Other farmhouses and country cottages built during the 1800s featured Victorian architectural designs. The Gothic Revival–style cottage was popularized as a country home during the 1850s. While later types of Victorian architecture, such as the ornate Second Empire and Queen Anne, were rarely used in farmhouses, Italianate styling—which features massive brackets under the eaves, a signature cupola, and tall windows with curved tops—was adapted for these structures between the 1850s and 1880s.

The barn, a quintessential country building, was built in various styles and sizes and constructed of wood, brick, or stone. Wooden examples were often painted white or red or were simply allowed to wear their natural finish. Unfortunately, many barns are now being torn down to make way for more modern facilities. But others are being lovingly restored and renovated into desirable dwellings. There are even companies that specialize in rescuing barns from the wrecking ball and setting them up elsewhere as homes. With their incredibly high ceilings, these structures make for spacious-feeling country retreats.

Other outbuildings associated with the farm include chicken coops, assorted sheds for tools and equipment, and in many cases a stable. Rural areas also feature other buildings that have residential potential today. Everything from old schoolhouses and grain mills to abandoned churches, carriage houses, and empty roadside shops are being restored as modern-day dwellings.

This small, rustic dwelling has been expanded over the years with a lean-to-addition off the back and another addition off one side. Filled with pioneer spirit, the original structure features square-hewn logs and a stone chimney.

Europe has its share of archetypal country homes as well. The styles of many of these, both inside and out, have been adopted in other parts of the world; such is the powerful hold that these enchanting old-world charmers have on our psyches. In England, the countryside is dotted with manor houses, thatched-roof cottages, and stone lodges. In days gone by, the manor house spoke of a family's prosperity, and country pursuits revolved around hunting and polo matches. Quaint cottages on the grounds or in nearby villages housed the hired help that kept the manor house running smoothly. Cozy dwellings of one and a half or two stories, these quintessential English cottages each typically sported a steeply pitched roof, diminutive diamond-paned windows, and timbered ceilings. Today, many of these serve as peaceful country getaways. The one thing the manor houses and diminutive cottages have always had in common is their close link to the surrounding landscape. Ivy and roses climb the walls of cottages, flower-draped arbors create smooth transitions between indoors and out, and bountiful gardens bring natural color right up to the back door. Constructed of timber, brick, or stone, these rural dwellings manifest natural color and texture that match the look of the countryside and give them a sense of belonging.

Left: *A European-style country home features weathered timber and a shake roof. The guest cottage, although much smaller, is every bit as enchanting as the main house. Notice how the two are visually linked by their accents of green. On the lawn, a pushcart filled with red blooms extends a friendly greeting.*
Below: *A log house and its outbuildings can be the perfect spot for different generations to come together on vacation. While the main house invites everyone to gather, the separate accommodations afford individuals some valuable quiet time.*

Pink roses climbing up the facade imbue this shingled cottage with a romantic air. A white picket fence completes the quaint picture.

modernized plumbing and the reconfiguration of interior space. Windows are often replaced, insulation and a heating system added, kitchens updated, old wood floors stripped of paint, and porches rebuilt. The list can go on and on, for any old house can be a continual work in progress, but the rewards of bringing a glorious old farmhouse back to life are immeasurable. The same can be said for old barns that are creatively transformed into roomy, open-living country homes and diminutive chicken coops that become comfy guest quarters, an artist's studio, an inviting pool house, or even a magical playhouse.

What about the country dwelling in the heart of the rural village or hamlet? Cozy little cottages can be found far and wide on treed lots in quiet settings that offer abundant opportunity to garden and become part of a close-knit community. Clapboard Victorians and shingled cottages built during the late nineteenth and early twentieth centuries can be altered considerably with a fresh coat of paint and personal spaces designed to meet your needs.

What happens when you've spent countless hours searching for that idyllic country home but have yet to discover the perfect property? Faced with such a situation, many decide to build. New country homes are being designed with the best qualities of vernacular style while incorporating modern-day amenities to ensure the utmost in comfort and an easy—even pampered—lifestyle. Federal-style Greek Revival, and Victorian architectural designs have all been reinterpreted for a fresh new look, yet they still blend harmoniously in rural settings. Homes in the Tudor Revival (also called English Medieval), Colonial Revival, and French Revival styles are other popular options for new builds in a rural setting. Above all, consider the location, landscape, and architectural designs of other buildings in the area to determine the best possible plan.

In France, a variety of cottage styles stand out. In mountainous areas, half-timbered cottages have predominated for centuries, while in the south of France, color-washed stone has long presided over the land. In other areas, such as the hillsides of wine country, stone houses rise up from the landscape. And in Provence, the limestone rubble used to construct homes typically displays soft colors reminiscent of the natural environment. Colorful shutters, window boxes filled with assorted blooms, and lace curtains complete the pretty picture in all regions.

The Rural Getaway

Rural dwellings come in assorted architectural styles. Old stone or clapboard farmhouses are being carefully restored with a sensitive eye on the past to maintain the integrity and simple beauty of the home. Major renovations include everything from structural or foundation repairs and new electrical systems and wiring to

Rural Exteriors

While the building site or the potential of a panoramic view is often the determining factor in the style of

Left and Bottom Left:
With a little fixing up, an old tool shed has been transformed into a secluded guest bedroom. The barn-red exterior enhances the country ambience. By painting the interior a pale cream color and selecting white bed linens, the owners have opened up the small space. Antique trunks provide efficient storage while making a decorative contribution at the same time. They help create a travel theme that is furthered by the globe and the airy white canopy reminiscent of mosquito netting. All the elements come together to whisk occupants away to the exotic locale of their dreams.

Rural Getaways

Right: *The landscape and natural terrain can lead to innovative design when building a rural retreat. Seen from the back, this fanciful getaway reveals the owner's desire for multi-level views. The modern interpretation of a Victorian turret is reminiscent of a tree house and is undoubtedly a favorite spot for everything from bird-watching to catching the sunrise.*

Bottom Right: *A Victorian Revival–style cottage built on a gentle slope wears a cheerful facade complete with whimsical trim. The amiable front porch allows plenty of opportunity for taking in the scenery, including the flower beds that line the brick walk. Should the weather take a turn for the worse, there's comfort to be found in the soothing sounds of raindrops splish-splashing on the painted metal roof.*

windows chosen for many a vacation home or cottage, when it comes to countryside retreats, the architectural style of the structure inevitably sets the tone these features. Given the fact that the countryside is dotted with numerous venerable older buildings, restoration work and the construction of new builds should be carried out with regard for the components of the designated style. For example, if you have a Greek Revival–style farmhouse with double-hung windows that need to be replaced for better insultation, use ones in the same style. Thanks to current offerings, you can have the look of yesteryear with the energy efficiency of today. Keep in mind that new windows can be custom-crafted to maintain the character of an older dwelling when stock windows won't fill the bill.

The numerous architectural salvage emporiums located in major cities across the country are yet

With one window opened wide to let in the breeze and sunlight streaming in through the floor-to-ceiling window and French doors, dining in this eat-in kitchen is practically an alfresco experience. Glass-front cabinetry mimics the look of the mullioned windows and doors, while white paneled walls create a peaceful backdrop. A glass vase and pitcher filled with fresh flowers bring the charms of the idyllic setting indoors.

another option when it comes to either building or restoring a rural retreat. Treasure troves of merchandise, these shops generally stock assorted windows, including the art glass and etched glass examples popular in Victorian architecture, as well as decorative exterior trim, lumber, porch columns, and all sorts of appropriate hardware.

A popular trend when it comes to window designs on older structures or new buildings that follow the letter of a particular architectural style is designing the front of the home in the prescribed fashion and then planning the back—that portion that is not seen from the road—to perfectly suit the owners needs. These features on the more private side of the home can take numerous different forms depending upon personal needs and preferences, but a double set of French doors leading out to a spacious and secluded patio or a large picture window taking advantage of a pleasing meadow view are among the more dramatic.

As with the style of windows, the material selected for a rural home's exterior takes its cue from architectural styling. The French-inspired cottage may be built of brick or stone, but the typical American farmhouse is best dressed in clapboard or vinyl siding that presents the appearance of clapboard. At the heart of the matter is the desire to have a country home that suits its surroundings, blends comfortably with the community, and affords you the opportunity to experience country living at its best.

Country Interiors

Your rural retreat should be casual and accommodating, conveying all the warmth and hospitality associated with a country decor. The concept of country, however, is multifaceted: there are many regional, ethnic, and even religious interpretations of the style. It can evoke

Left: *White walls and bleached plank flooring allow furnishings and accessories to shine. A Shaker-inspired bed is dressed in coral pink and a medium blue for a dash of color, while the plaid rug contributes pattern and texture. Vintage suitcases, piled high, serve as a nightstand.*

the homespun charm found in the North American farmhouse, the timeless elegance and enchantment of the English cottage, or the joie de vivre sensation of the French country cottage, complete with rugged textures and vibrant prints.

When it comes to the color palette for a North American-style farmhouse, white and other neutral hues are popular choices for a clean, contemporary look. But don't let that stop you from painting your home in the stronger colors long associated with rural dwellings, such as red, green, mustard, or navy blue.

Above: *Blue and white, long a favorite color combination, creates a clean, pure look in this tranquil bedroom. Crisp white walls and plank flooring flatter a striking bed with a fabric-covered headboard and matching bed skirt.*

The spirit of the farm-
house is clearly conveyed
in this pantry that now
functions as a mudroom.
Green beadboard paneling
and the cabinetry's black
hinges and pulls recall the
early twentieth-century
period when a large
number of working farms
dotted the landscape.
Flagstone flooring is practical as well as beautiful,
and an old church pew
comes in handy for pulling
off boots. Wire baskets,
iron hooks for jackets, and
old tools displayed on the
wall evoke images of a
rural lifestyle.

Left: *Wallpaper in a soft apricot hue sporting a diminutive checked pattern combines with botanical prints and floral bedding to infuse this bedroom with romantic airs. Images of sleeping in a meadow or flower garden are called to mind courtesy of the color- ful blooms. White trim provides pleasant contrast, drawing the eye toward the octagonal window and the trees beyond.*

Right: *A jumble of patterns, textures, and collectibles fills this farm- house kitchen with cheer. The happy medley is a success, thanks to a common thread—color. A blue and yellow theme pervades, creating a sunny and uplifting setting.*

Right: *Much of the joy in setting up a rural retreat comes from the knowledge that furniture need not be perfect and that second-hand goods can be freshened up with a creative paint job. Here, a sturdy pine table is enlivened with chairs painted in an uplifting array of blues, greens, and yellows. Notice how the chairs pop against the subtle hues of the backdrop.*

Bottom and Opposite: *Having fun is what a country getaway is all about, so why not set the mood with whimsical decor? Guests will certainly enjoy their meal in this boisterous dining room. The space is filled with elements that one would expect to find outdoors, such as a weathervane, a collection of birdhouses, and a picket fence (here in the form of a bench back). The sense of unpredictability is furthered by a chair hanging on the wall and playing host to a bunch of wildflowers in an old milk bottle. A colorful assortment of painted chairs pulls up to the table, while a mustard corner cabinet holds prized objects amassed over the years. Backed by crisp white walls and gray-green trim, the painted furniture comes to life.*

Selecting white paint for walls does, however, have the advantage of allowing handsome wood and painted furnishings or collections to take center stage. White will also provide a distraction-free backdrop in a farmhouse where the surrounding fields become the focal point via large windows and a generous supply of French doors. When combined with deep or muted shades for trim-work, white can evoke the spirit of Shaker style. In contrast, painting walls a soft yellow, sage green, or light blue adds a certain warmth that makes for cozier rooms. Darker colors can be introduced for contrast through assorted decorative accessories.

Wallpaper has immense decorative potential. Mini prints, floral patterns, and stripes will contribute to the farmhouse feeling, but designs with a white or pale

neutral background are preferable to ensure that rooms remain light and airy. Stripes and mini prints are especially at home in living areas, while florals set a romantic tone in the bedroom. In the kitchen or bath, depending upon your personal taste, a half-paneled wall (wood-toned or painted) used in tandem with wallpaper forms a decorative backdrop for crisp, white fixtures and white, honey pine, or painted cabinetry.

Stenciling is another way of introducing color and establishing a country tone that pays homage to the past. In nineteenth-century New England, itinerant artisans would use this technique to paint designs in the homes of farmers and other families. This process was desirable as it was much more affordable than wallpaper. Today, whether it is used to adorn a bedroom wall with willow trees (a common motif of yesteryear) or to give a living room an eye-catching border of pineapples (the colonial symbol for hospitality), stenciling will play up the country flavor of a setting and infuse the home with a sense of tradition.

Flooring in a farmhouse is usually made of wood. Wide pine planks, which contribute an aged, rugged look, are often favored for their understated beauty. If

Above: *For a signature touch, plank flooring has been painted with a colorful border of flowers, barnyard animals, dogs, and cats. Here's proof positive that a little creativity can transform almost any surface into a folk-art masterpiece. For good measure, a fitting collection of primitive pull toys is displayed along the playful design.*

Left: *A neutral backdrop is the perfect foil for select country touches that infuse this bedroom with style. An iron bed with brass trim comes to life outfitted with a jaunty checkered spread and plaid pillows. Look carefully at the pine bedside table and note the stenciled design and the miniature chairs displayed atop the books. It's the thoughtful details that make this room a welcoming retreat.*

A farmhouse bath, complete with a vintage-style sink and tub, takes its cue from the garden just outside the window. Flowery wallpaper covers the upper portion of the walls, as well as the ceiling, while matching curtains hang at the window. Color-coordinated towels and accessories give the bath a polished look, and natural wood flooring contributes warmth.

you're building a new country home, recycled lumber can help make the structure look as if it has stood the test of time. Painted wood floors are another option. A painted floor can be stenciled or treated to a special paint technique such as spattering to give it a signature touch. Other options include painting wooden floorboards with a checkerboard pattern for a classic look or adorning a stairwell with a trompe l'oeil runner. In the kitchen and bathroom, tile or resilient flooring with a checkered pattern will contribute lots of casual country style. Try a combination of ocher and deep blue to infuse such spaces with subdued color.

Other components that help create a fitting backdrop include a wood-burning stove or a fireplace with a wood, stone, or brick surround in the living room and or kitchen. A humble mantel made from hand-hewn timber can be an amiable resting spot for a gathering of country collectibles. Consider, too, the elegance imparted by adding other architectural elements, such as bull's-eye window moldings, a handsome wood staircase, or an art glass window in that perfect spot. Overhead, hand-hewn beams radiate hearty country appeal.

Country decorating is, above all, a very flexible way of outfitting an inviting and comfortable home. Fortunately, you don't have to own a cottage or manor house outside London to enjoy all the charms of English country–style decorating. Simply put, it's all about layering: color and texture form a backdrop to which you add pattern, plump furnishings, and cherished objects galore. The end result is a warm and homey setting that looks as though it has gradually evolved over the years—in fact, most have. Part of the joy of a cottage decor is that it is in a constant though subtle state of flux, welcoming into the mix new finds and prized possessions—those must-have treasures found on trips and in off-the-beaten-path antique shops.

When it comes to setting an English country tone—whether it be in a simple little cottage in northern Ontario, an old stone carriage house in New England, or a timber-framed thatched cottage in the English countryside—the best place to start is with

Reminiscent of a colonial keeping room, this striking living space combines rugged texture with soft color to achieve beautiful results. Situated against a sage green wall, the brick hearth becomes a focal point, complete with an eye-catching collection of pewter plates and candlesticks. Comfortable upholstered furnishings soften the rustic airs of log walls and a wood-beamed ceiling.

Right: *In typical English country fashion, a medley of furnishings and fabrics has been called upon to design this cozy refuge. Wallpaper with a lilac print lends old-world charm, and identical white iron beds contribute a cheery note. At the window seat, gauzy curtains and a floral-patterned cushion create a dreamy setting.*

Opposite Bottom: *A formal French country tone pervades this elegant living room. Florals, stripes, and checks happily coexist in the backdrop and furnishings, creating a look that seems to have evolved over time. At the heart of the room, a small fireplace casts a warming glow, while the mantel provides a resting spot for framed photographs and other cherished items. Above the hearth, a built-in compartment houses a television that can be closed off when not in use. The other side of the cupboard door features a gilt mirror—a more traditional accoutrement for the area above a fireplace.*

color. Soft hues such as pastels are a fitting backdrop for warm honey pine chests, dressers, and scrubbed-top tables. Light yellow, rose, or apricot paint on walls tends to brighten small rooms and spaces with diminutive cottage windows. Pastels also create a pleasing effect in rooms with an abundance of natural texture displayed in timbered or stone walls, wood-beamed ceilings, and plank floors. Last but not least, pastels blend harmoniously with the floral-print upholstery so prevalent in English country decors and fill interiors with a breath of fresh springtime air, even when skies are gray. Deeper colors, such as shades of brown (in wood-toned paneling), green, yellow, blue, claret, or teal blue, are

better suited to larger or more formal rooms. These strong hues make flattering backdrops for mahogany and other dark wood furnishings.

Wallpaper can be used in the living room and dining room of the English country–style cottage, but it is perhaps most often associated with the snug under-the-eaves bedroom. Small floral designs, ivy prints, stripes, and mini prints unify quirky spaces with slanted ceilings and those character-imbuing nooks and crannies.

Plank or hardwood strip flooring should be used in living areas and layered with small and large oriental, needlepoint, or natural-fiber rugs. In bedrooms, wood floors can be left natural or painted and stenciled. If you prefer to have some softness underfoot, install wall-to-wall carpeting in a soft hue or in a deeper shade of the color used on the walls. In the English country kitchen and bath, terra-cotta tiles, brick flooring, or a resilient flooring with the look of tile or brick is appropriate. Slate will also convey the right tone in the kitchen.

A small fireplace in the living room can be accessorized with a timber mantel or a colorful tile surround. Wood beams added to the ceiling will establish a more authentic look, and built-in shelves will allow plenty of room to display books and a host of collectibles. And there's nothing like a glass conservatory—the quintessential English garden room—to enable year-round enjoyment of the outdoors.

Just as the palette of the English cottage reflects the lush green countryside and colorful floral gardens, the French country interior takes its cues from fields of lavender, cloudless blue skies, cheerful poppies and sunflowers, and clays found in the sun-baked earth. Creating a French country ambience entails combining earthy colors with rugged textures. Old plaster walls or wallboard can be color-washed in a yellow ocher or pale terra-cotta to give living rooms, dining rooms, and kitchens French country airs. Keep in mind that neutral painted walls serve as the perfect foil for vibrant French blue trim on moldings, window frames, and doors. Bedrooms give way to pale shades of lavender, rose, ivory, silver-blue, or cream. In kitchens and baths, tile makes a decorative statement through both color and pattern. But tile is not just another pretty face in these areas. Part of the reason it has so long been a part of French country decor is because of its highly functional nature. Half-tiled walls, a tiled backsplash, and a tiled stove surround can all be used to infuse a kitchen with French country flavor.

If wallpaper is desired, you can't go astray with a checkered pattern or a toile de Jouy, both of which set the right mood in red and white or blue and white. Checks make for an upbeat country kitchen (the heart of the French country home), while a toile pattern creates a casual yet sophisticated living or dining room

Left: *A colorful sink featuring strong blues and yellows injects a French country flair into a kitchen. The lively design boasts everything from roosters and cows to fruits and leaves—all appropriate for a rural setting.*

and an equally captivating bedroom. Small floral patterns in shades of green, blue, lavender, or rose will add a soft touch to bedrooms.

For flooring, terra-cotta tiles—available in various shapes and sizes—or slate can be used in kitchens and living areas. These floors are often left bare to let the beauty of the natural material shine forth. Resilient flooring that looks like tile or stone is a cost-effective alternative. Wood flooring topped with natural-fiber rugs will also set a French country mood. And such architectural features as stone walls, timbered ceilings, and a tiled hearth contribute the rugged texture long considered a hallmark of French country interiors.

Rural Furnishings

Calling to mind images of cozy comfort and practicality, the American farmhouse is best furnished with a medley of pieces that are sturdy, easy to care for, and straightforward in style. Oak, chestnut, pine, and cherry furnishings are ideal since these wood tones look striking against a white or neutral backdrop. Antiques shops and auctions are excellent sources for vintage wood furnishings, but several noted manufacturers have lines geared toward country decorating.

As you outfit your cottage, consider the various benefits of certain furnishings as well as their aesthetic connotations. Imagine yourself being soothed by the

gentle motion of a wooden rocking chair. Or picture yourself settled into the embrace of a traditional wing-back chair with a patterned quilt wrapped around your legs. How about bringing a drop-leaf table—a natural for conserving space—into the ensemble? Other pieces suited for living areas include camel-back sofas and plump easy chairs. In the dining area, a harvest table is the perfect spot for a scrumptious meal.

Upholstered pieces sporting sprightly checks, solid stripes, and refreshing floral patterns inject a jubilant tone. If you opt for solid-color fabrics on sofas and chairs, accessorize these pieces with colorful print pillows and patterned throws that bear at least a touch of the upholstery's hue. As a result, you'll have a happy jumble of designs that nonetheless relate to one another. Go with heavyweight fabrics treated for stain resistance if you want something that will wear like iron. If you like to shake things up a little and need variety from time to time, opt for slipcovers; it's a snap to alter the whole look of a room by simply taking them off and putting different ones on.

Painted furnishings, from chests to chairs to tables, have long been associated with a rural lifestyle. Add a painted bench to the entryway—what better place to pull off damp or muddy boots or sneakers after a long walk through a dew-filled meadow? Place a bench in the living room and outfit it with cushions for comfortable extra seating. Or, for something unexpected, pull a bench up to one side of a harvest table to replace ordinary chairs. Traditionally used for garden seating and picnicking, benches have the added bonus of conjuring images of the outdoors when used inside. Within the cottage, they not only offer a place to sit a spell, but provide a convenient spot for stacking books and magazines or showing off a favorite collection. Painted trunks, step-back cupboards, and assorted tables are other fetching additions. Picture a harvest table surrounded by ladder-back chairs with rungs of alternating blue and yellow paint. In the bedroom, try a chest of drawers bearing a hand-painted bucolic scene.

Shaker-style furnishings and wicker pieces can be successfully blended into a farmhouse decor. Even a

singular piece, such as a Shaker rocking chair, imparts elegant simplicity and beautiful craftsmanship. Introducing a set of Shaker tape-seat chairs with red and white woven listing can enliven a plain wooden plank table while maintaining a sense of simplicity. Wicker—casual, light, and airy—is always befitting a country home and is especially lovely when used in a farmhouse bedroom. A bed, a chest, or just a comfy, cushioned chair in wicker situated by the bedroom window for enjoying the view can be a pleasant reminder of days gone by.

For kitchens, painted white cabinets, in keeping with a more modern or minimalist interpretation of country style, make a room seem bright and fresh. Knotty pine, oak, and cherry cabinetry have more rustic and Shakerlike qualities. To complement white cabinetry, consider a tile or butcher-block countertop. Wood-tone cabinets, on the other hand, will benefit

A paean to tranquility, this bedroom makes the most of natural light with neutral hues and subtle patterns. A minimum of furniture— an antique armoire and a simple footlocker—ensures a serene space.

Left: *A lot has been packed into a narrow space to achieve a highly serviceable, as well as visually pleasing, kitchen. The setup includes both butcher-block and marble surfaces to accommodate different cooking and baking activities. Above and below the counters, various painted cabinets, whose dark hues stand out against the pale yellow-green walls, provide plenty of storage and even some display space.*

Above: *Serene white walls and plank flooring set the stage for charming fixtures and accessories in this farmhouse-style bath. An old claw-foot tub encourages relaxing soaks, while a simple wooden chair keeps towels close at hand. Instead of using a stock vanity or a reproduction pedestal sink, the owner has incorporated a marble-top commode that has been outfitted with a basin, thereby giving the room heightened, vintage flavor. The round braided rug and the art glass window supply touches of color to the primarily neutral setting.*

from a colorful laminate counter that lends contrast. A small porcelain-top, scrubbed-top, or round oak table in the kitchen will make for cozy family meals.

Cabinets in the bathroom follow the same guidelines as those in the kitchen. To play up the country ambience, encase the tub in a beadboard surround. If you have the space, bring in a simple wooden chair and pile it high with towels in a rainbow of colors. If space is at a premium, give a milking stool a second career as a keeper of towels or bath accessories. Of course, a peg rack is one of the most space-efficient means for keeping towels on hand.

Unlike the North American farmhouse look, where less is more and rooms are furnished for simplicity and utility, the English country house proclaims that you can't have enough of a good thing. Prevailing fashions never took precedence in the English country cottage. Rather, furniture was passed from one generation to the next, and upholstery worn thin on chairs and sofas was simply masked with slipcovers. Favorite objects and collections, always a source of homey comfort, found their way into every nook and cranny.

Opposite: *In this bedroom, stone walls are softened by a bed outfitted with loads of floral pillows, quilts, and comforters. True to the nature of English country style, an abundance of cherished objects—namely dollhouse furnishings—are on display. The pint-size furnishings offer a playful nod to the typical small scale of cottage rooms.*

Above: *Cozy comfort and floral motifs are hallmarks of English country style. In this favorite corner, an embracing wing chair, a plump ottoman, and a Victorian pole lamp create an inviting spot for curling up with a cup of tea and a good book.*

Left: *This exuberant kitchen, artfully cluttered in true English country fashion, makes the most wonderful use of available space. China, framed prints, fresh flowers, and even a vintage birdcage have all found their way into the splendid setting.*

tight grouping of photographs in pewter frames of different styles and sizes. Salvaged objects can find their place in the bedroom, too. Why not give yourself the sensation of sleeping in the midst of an English garden by incorporating a headboard fashioned from a wrought-iron grille that once graced a garden gate?

The English country–style kitchen, in typical old-world fashion, is often "unfitted." Eschewing the utilitarian look, this type of kitchen boasts a more furnished appearance with the help of freestanding dressers or cupboards for storage and display. A more contemporary take on the style calls for built-in cabinetry with a warm pine finish and porcelain drawer pulls. Wall-hung open shelving can also be used to take the place of classic cupboards. Another alternative is custom-crafted cabinetry with a pastel painted finish.

For the bath, look to a pedestal sink and claw-foot tub to evoke the sensation of a past era. Introduce a pine wall-hung cupboard with glass doors or an old chest to store towels and toiletries.

For those who long for the old-world ambience of a more rugged rural lifestyle, French country decorating answers the call. Elegant rusticity results from blending earth colors with peasant-style furnishings crafted for country life.

The armoire is the quintessential French country furniture piece. Made centuries ago to hold a bride's dowry, the armoire has become a multifunctional piece that can take up residence in almost any room. Use an armoire in the living room as an entertainment cabinet or in the bedroom for linens and clothing. Frequently made of walnut, cherry, or other fruit woods, antique armoires can fetch top dollar. Fortunately, talented craftspeople and furniture manufacturers produce authentic-looking reproductions.

Other furnishings with distinct French styling include banquettes, rush-seat chairs (which can be used in the dining room or living room), rush-seat settees, and low buffets. Sofas and easy chairs upholstered in colorful French Provençal prints consisting of small floral, geometric, paisley, or fruit patterns also fit the bill.

Architectural salvage opens up a world of possibilities when decorating a cottage retreat. Here, swirling wrought-iron grilles that once adorned garden gates have been reincarnated as a headboard and footboard. Fresh flowers complete the garden ambience.

To create the ambience of a traditional English country cottage today, combine furnishings old and new that will merge the right look with the sought-after comfort level. A large honey pine hutch in the living room, kitchen, or dining room makes a superb home for a china collection. Incorporate small wood tables and Windsor chairs into the living room along with a sink-down sofa and overstuffed easy chairs. Wood furnishings tend to be oak, mahogany, or, for more cottagelike appeal, a mellow pine. Bedrooms are often bedecked with painted furniture. Soft pastel beds, dressers, and chests of drawers can be enhanced with hand-painted or stenciled floral motifs. A four-poster, canopy, or painted iron bed is also welcome, along with a dressing table, a tiled washstand, or a round bedside table covered with a floor-length cloth and filled with a

French country–style bedrooms often play host to old brass or iron beds complete with headboards and footboards, which suggest understated elegance. Sleigh beds, admired for their soft, sloping lines, offer loads of old-world appeal. Another option is a wood-finished bed with delicate floral carvings. A painted bed with a scalloped headboard and a dainty white linen coverlet is yet another way to go. And don't overlook the come-hither appeal of a toile de Jouy canopy suspended from the ceiling over the bed.

Kitchen furnishings include signature items, such as a metal baker's rack, an armoire, freestanding walnut cupboards, a square wooden table accompanied by rush-seat chairs, or a round metal table with bistro chairs. The bath pays tribute to the past with a vintage-style sink and tub. Skirt a white pedestal sink with a yellow and blue Provençal print for an uplifting dose of summery color, and enhance the resulting airy sensation by housing the tub in crisp, white latticework.

Accessories and Collectibles

The essence of any version of country style lies in its celebration of a history that inspires our deep appreciation and affection. And what better way to revel in and exalt the past by filling the cottage with decorative

What do a wooden rocking horse, an ironstone pitcher, a barber's pole, and a collection of candlesticks have in common? They're all pieces of the American past. Collected on treasure hunts at country auctions and roadside antiques shops, these beloved objects give the living room a personal note as well as a sense of rural history.

accessories and objects that evoke feelings of nostalgia? Regardless of whether your favorite objects once held pride of place in a rural dwelling or served a more humble utilitarian function, handmade items, along with select antiques and collectibles, are at the very heart of country decorating.

In an American farmhouse–style getaway, a warm first impression can be achieved with something as simple as a wreath on the front door. A floral, grapevine, evergreen, or pinecone wreath, selected according to the season, will imbue your entrance with hospitality and hint at the casual country-style rooms waiting beyond the door. For living areas with wood floors, add a colorful rug or two to introduce color and texture. Needlepoint and rag rugs bring the spirit of country style to virtually any room in the house.

The best-dressed windows are often the ones with a simple yet lovely window treatment. Depending upon the view, there may be certain windows you decide to leave bare. But in those places where some sort of window dressing is desired, consider lined tab curtains, tailored drapes, or shutters painted white. For bedrooms, lace or muslin panels or perhaps a cotton print will serve you well. Remember that a simple window dressing can also be elegant, especially when you add decorative wood or metal rods. In the kitchen, a spirited check, floral, stripe, or mini print lends a family-friendly room abundant country style. Inject a personal touch by fashioning café curtains from former linens.

Table lamps with a black iron or pottery base can be reminiscent of days gone by. Outfit lamps with colorful patterned or glass shades. Use a kerosene lamp wired for electricity on the bedside table, and don't forget the iron or wood chandelier with curved arms for shedding light over the kitchen or dining table. Wall sconces with decorative glass globes or petite fabric shades contribute style in the bath.

Enhance walls with lively quilts, paintings of rural scenes, or perhaps a collection of barn photographs. Mount a birdhouse on a wall as a reminder of the wildlife outside, or jazz up the staircase with an assortment of old washboards, arranging them on the wall so that they ascend with the steps. In the bedroom, pepper

a wall with an array of needlepoint samplers. Hang an old-fashioned bed warmer, or simply rest one up against the wall in a corner. In the living area or dining space, give an empty corner a healthy dose of traditional country charm by filling it with an antique butter churner. In a similar vein, recall earlier times by incorporating a wooden spinning wheel as a decorative accent.

One of the elements that draws us to the countryside in the first place is its generous offering of nature's gifts. Take advantage of these when decorating the interior. For instance, scatter freshly picked flowers throughout the cottage. Not only will they enhance rooms with festive displays of color, but they'll infuse the entire cottage with the sweet scents of the outdoors. Old-fashioned jelly jars, milk bottles, and tin pails and watering cans all make hospitable homes for these blooms. And don't forget the decorative appeal of fresh produce. Who doesn't like to be greeted by a bowl of assorted fruits at the coffee table or dining table? In autumn, a basket of gourds makes a colorful centerpiece.

Other objects with country flavor include baskets, always appreciated for their practical as well as decorative qualities; stoneware crocks; white ironstone pitchers; vintage enamelware with marbled or mottled patterns in

Opposite: *Arranging a collection of vintage enamelware and time-worn kitchen utensils on shelves and peg racks has dramatic impact in this warm country kitchen. Even the old enameled stove becomes an impromptu display spot for a vintage bread bin and teakettle.*

Above: *Understated elegance is the result when antique stoneware is artfully showcased on a wood tabletop. Iron candlesticks give the picture-perfect vignette a sense of balance, while the painting behind repeats the earthy hues of the jugs.*

such colors as red, blue, green, gray, and brown; folk art pieces; cowbells; old mixing bowls; and kitchen utensils with cheerful colored wood handles. Group like objects to form a collection, but be selective about the items you choose to amass. The weekend home should be comfortable, not overly cluttered.

In contrast, clutter—an artful clutter, that is—almost seems to be key when decorating in the English country style. A happy hodgepodge of furnishings and collectibles tied together by color, texture, or scale makes for particularly cozy rooms.

Windows—especially the smaller examples often found in rural cottages—are an important source of natural lighting. To maximize light and pleasing views, a chintz valance or lovely chintz curtains that can be looped back are the perfect English country–style accessories. Lace panels and Austrian shades exude the romantic airs of an English country setting; for something a bit more formal, floor-length patterned drapes on decorative rods convey traditional elegance.

Lamps and lighting fixtures take their cue from classical shapes and forms or more romantic designs. For example, urn-shaped or candlestick lamps complement an English country decor, as do simpler pottery or metal-based lamps with jaunty, pleated shades. Gilt wall sconces and chandeliers are quite fitting in the dining room, and antique or reproduction fixtures are well suited to the kitchen and bath.

Choose artwork associated with the English countryside, such as hunting prints and landscape scenes. An assortment of botanical prints may be just the right finishing touch for a flowery guest bedroom. In the living room, set an antique silver or china tea service at one end of a coffee table or in the middle of a side table. Not only do such pieces make stunning ornaments, but they convey a sense of hospitality and pay tribute to a time-honored British tradition. Extend the theme by filling a built-in corner cupboard with a colorful jumble of mismatched teacups and teapots. Staffordshire figures, vintage ironstone pottery, British porcelain and enamelware, and blue and white china are other accessories that come into play in different rooms. And as with any country cottage, framed family photos, books, and flower-filled pitchers will contribute to a lived-in feeling.

French country interiors call upon bold texture in decorative accessories, and cottages in this style abound with stone, terra-cotta, and wood. When it comes to windows, bamboo shades make for an earthy window dressing, while elegant lace panels, long a hallmark of French country style, provide an airier feeling. Pull shades can be used underneath lace curtains for privacy, or the lace itself can serve as an undercurtain with striking Provençal or toile drapes on handsome black iron rods.

Wrought-iron chandeliers, table lamps, and floor lamps as well as wicker and pottery-based lamps are employed in the French country–style cottage. Black, a crisp white, or a colorful print used on lampshades will set these features off quite strikingly.

Many of the objects that exude French country charm reflect the French passion for food. Beautiful dishware and cooking implements not only serve functional purposes but boast tremendous decorative power. With this in mind, go to town when outfitting the kitchen and dining area. Let dishes, mugs, and canisters bask in the limelight by using open shelving, where these items can be on display day and night. For authentic French flavor, incorporate a *panetière*, a traditional wall-hung device for storing bread. Hang gleaming copper pots and pans on overhead racks, which not only present a space-efficient storage solution but allow these warm-looking cooking devices to shine where all can see. Further draw the eye upward by dangling dried herbs and flowers from ceiling beams in true French country style. In the dining area, fill a plate rack with colorful faience or mount an array of festive dishes on the wall as art. Other ingredients for French country

ambience include wireware baskets and egg racks, glass bottles and jars in colors reminiscent of the Mediterranean, and European enamelware with floral, checkered, or striped patterns.

Don't overlook the power of scent to transport you to rural France. Place small bowls of potpourri in various rooms, and let the tantalizing aroma waft throughout the cottage. Lavender in particular will conjure images of the French countryside. Said to have soothing powers, this herb is most appropriate in the bedroom. You might even want to tuck lavender sachets into dresser drawers—this small gesture will go a long way. In the bath, consider arranging lavender-scented candles around the tub to enhance the feeling of relaxation.

Natural accents give this country kitchen its charm. A basket of flowers by the door, a vase of cheerful blooms on the table, and a bowl of fresh fruit are all simple yet thoughtful gestures that inject a note of hospitality. For a crowning touch, dried herbs and flowers have been hung overhead in typical French country style.

Mountain and Woodland Retreats

THERE IS SOMETHING MYSTICAL, EVEN SPIRITUAL, ABOUT the forest primeval. Surrounded by towering evergreens, white birch, or myriad hardwoods, a cottage retreat nestled in the woods or in the embrace of a mountainside is at one with nature. With the blue sky above and a carpet of pine needles, moss, or leaves below, there is a sense of calm—a feeling of serenity and well-being that renews the spirit. The mountain or woodland retreat is a peaceful haven where technology, industry, and commerce are left behind for such invigorating and relaxing pursuits as hiking in the woods, lighting a fire in the hearth, and slipping out to the porch to admire the sunrise or gaze upon the stars.

A Style Is Born

There are various architectural interpretations of a rustic retreat, but the elements that they tend to have in common are the use of natural materials and a location and construction sensitive to the immediate surroundings. Rustic style is generally associated with furnishings crafted from trees, twigs, bark, and antlers, but it does not mean primitive or "roughing it." Quite the contrary—it can be exceedingly beautiful, artistic, and awe-inspiring.

In North America, the earliest rustic homes were the log cabins of Native Americans and, later, French, Swedish and German settlers who arrived in the 1600s. The next wave of log-home building came during the pioneer era. Settlers moving west built cabins along the St. Lawrence River, and the Great Lakes, down into the American South and

Midwest, in California and British Columbia, and in Texas as temporary shelters until larger, more permanent homes, as well as outbuildings for animals, could be built.

The humble log home had a big influence on the rustic camps and lodges built throughout the eastern and western parts of North America during the late nineteenth century. For the most part, the camps consisted of a main lodge, surrounding cottages, a separate building for dining, and various maintenance buildings. The style was lovingly described in a little book, *Adventures in the Wilderness* (1867) by William H.H. Murray, which glorified the Adirondack Mountains region of New York State and the outdoor sports that could be enjoyed in that setting. Within a few short decades, railroad transportation made the trek to the mountains easier, and hotels sprang up at a fast and furious pace to accommodate growing numbers of hunters and fishermen. For those who wanted their very own little cabin in the woods, an 1889 book, *Log Cabins and Cottages: How to Build and Furnish Them*, by William Wicks, offered approximately twenty plans for log dwellings suited to the Adirondacks.

Lavish resorts quickly followed the hotel boom. Before long, the Vanderbilts, Morgans, and Rockefellers were buying huge parcels of land on which to build their own Adirondack camps. Among the architects who set a precedent for this regional style was William West Durant. Having spent time in Europe, Durant was guided by his passion for the Swiss chalet, a design well suited to a mountainous region known for its cold climate and riveting scenery. Durant designed several of what came to be known as the "great camps" in the Adirondacks—including Alfred G. Vanderbilt's Sagamore. Not only were the cottages and various other buildings designed and constructed to blend with the natural surroundings, but they were furnished with chairs, tables, and beds crafted from logs, twigs, and birch bark and embellished with pinecones, acorns, and mosaic twigwork.

With the late-nineteenth-century penchant for getting back to nature, other notable architects journeyed to the Adirondacks and built camps that reflected or combined some of the design elements seen in

log cabins of the American West, English half-timber cottages, Victorian villas, Alpine chalets, and even Japanese architecture. During the early 1900s, Adirondack-style architecture made its way across the continent via plan books for rustic retreats.

The Alpine chalet, one of the architectural influences often detected in Adirondack camps, was actually proposed for country houses decades earlier. Andrew Jackson Downing's 1850 plan book, *The Architecture of Country Houses*, featured several Swiss cottages. Downing professed that these chalets should be built in "bold and mountainous" sites or "at the bottom of a wooded hill." With their signature horizontal wood planking, pitched roofs, broad overhangs with brackets, decorative carved balconies, large porches, and colorful shutters, chalets were not only picturesque but also ideally suited to climates with significant snowfall. During the late nineteenth century and the early part of the twentieth century, various interpretations of the Alpine

Constructed with logs and bedecked with green trim, these cottages sport rustic, camplike airs. A similarly styled gazebo is suitable for both quiet contemplation and summertime celebrations.

chalet appeared in the Adirondacks, western Canada, and the western United States, especially in Montana's Glacier National Park.

The halcyon days of the great camps faded after two world wars and the Great Depression. In the Adirondacks, a handful of the large camps remain, although their property has been greatly reduced. A few operate as hotels or luxury resorts, such as The Point, once the summer home of William Rockefeller. Camp Sagamore on Raquette Lake has been restored by a nonprofit group and is open during the summer and early autumn for tours, lectures, and a limited number of guests.

The renewed interest in rustic style these past few decades has seen older buildings restored and new vacation homes built in wooded regions across the United States and Canada. While the vernacular may be state-of-the-art in terms of modern amenities and architectural designs may have a contemporary edge, the focus—being at one with the natural landscape—never waivers.

Rustic Exteriors

The site ultimately dictates the layout of a rustic cottage. Owners tend to take the best possible advantage of views by investing in fine-quality windows. Another goal is that the natural landscape be disturbed as little as possible. As a result, exteriors are usually designed to blend in with the natural environment.

There are several choices available for the exterior of a rustic retreat. Logs are extremely popular, and industry experts calculate that between twenty-five and thirty thousand new log homes are built each year. While some of these act as vacation homes, a great many now serve as year-round residences. They can be composed of red cedar, lodgepole pine, redwood, white cedar, Ponderosa pine, white pine, cypress, or spruce. Because these soft woods are easy to cut and adapt to various shapes, they are generally preferred for log-home building.

Whether a dwelling is constructed of rounded logs or half-logs is a matter of individual choice and

aesthetics; it depends upon the desired look, especially from the inside. Some rustic homes use log siding—boards that have been rounded to give the appearance of logs. There are also peeled and unpeeled logs. Most logs used in recent home constructions are peeled, but for a truly rustic look, some people opt for logs that have been "skip-peeled," a method of removing bark but leaving mottled traces of cambium (a layer of sapwood) behind. Log homes also differ from one another in respect to the orientation of the logs forming the exterior. These can be horizontal, vertical, or even a combination of both. The typical log dwelling relies upon a horizontal placement of logs, but some striking versions incorporate vertically oriented logs in the first story and horizontal ones for the upper story.

The majority of log homes employ dovetailed or saddle-notched joints, but the possibilities don't stop there. On the exterior, log ends can be pointed, appear rounded and project slightly from the exterior walls, or manifest a four-point diamond design.

Opposite: *This mountain retreat overlooking a stream was planned and built with careful consideration of the natural landscape. The log exterior blends in unobtrusively with the surrounding environment, and the spacious decks have been constructed around existing trees so as not to disturb them.*
Above: *This quaint cottage in the woods sports a fitting forest green paint job. For a whimsical touch, the entrance has been embellished with carved trim and a sunburst design.*

Other types of rustic cottages are constructed with board-and-batten siding, board-and-rough-channel siding, or cedar shingles. Board-and-batten has definite cottage appeal, and it can wear a natural finish or a coat of paint. Board-and-rough-channel siding is similar to board-and-batten except that the vertical wood planks have a rougher finish, thereby exhibiting a more primitive look. Cedar shingles or cedar shakes are often stained or allowed to weather to a soft gray.

Decorative exterior embellishments include stonework (in the foundation, porch, and chimney), birch bark, twigwork, massive logs, and colorful accents on doors, windows frames, or shutters. Fanciful carvings on porches and the use of art glass windows also enhance exteriors without detracting from the landscape.

Windows can be a sizable investment in revamping a rustic cottage or building a new one, but they are crucial to the design as they open the home to the outdoors, which floods rooms with natural light and fresh air, provides spectacular views, and makes small rooms seem larger. Windows help define the exterior by giving it character, expressing a certain style, or demonstrating a fresh take on a rustic design.

Even in a harsh climate, large windows can be energy-efficient, thanks to thermal-pane glass. Popular window styles for rustic cottages include double-hung and casement windows, French doors leading out onto a deck, large picture or fixed-glass windows (flanked by smaller windows that open for ventilation), and smaller, often fanciful windows in elliptical or diamond shapes.

Rustic Interiors

Like the exterior, the interior of the modern-day woodland cottage pays tribute to the great outdoors. Taking its cue from the surrounding views, a room can display elegant rusticity or a simpler beauty that allows natural texture to speak for itself. Design elements often include an efficient and convenient use of space, dual-purpose built-ins, and a fireplace—the quintessential focal point in a woodland home.

Interior walls are often made up of barn-board paneling, board-and-channel paneling, thin-strip bead-board paneling (which can be painted or treated to a natural or deeper wood finish), knotty pine boards, or rugged pine planking. While beadboard and planking are usually placed vertically, many owners opt for a horizontal pattern that contributes visual interest. Barn-board, knotty pine boards, and pine planking, all available in different widths from lumber mills and architectural emporiums, can contribute to the decor via their wood tones and graining. In homes constructed with rounded logs, interior walls naturally mirror the facade.

The trend is to decorate the living areas of woodland and mountain retreats in such strong hues as reds and greens in order to offset wood-finished walls. Bedrooms, however, tend to be lighter, making use of painted or wallpapered plasterboard. Neutral or pastel colors blend beautifully with colorful quilts, Native American blankets, and checkered Hudson Bay or Beacon blankets. Lighter colors also visually expand bedrooms that may have small windows and, hence, reduced natural lighting.

The essence of a woodland retreat can be created in any setting through a select use of color and pattern. Here, a refined rusticity has been achieved with a wing chair and ottoman upholstered in a Native American print, a striped rug, a wooden coffee table that shows off its natural graining, and a red leather sofa accessorized with toss pillows that link it to the chair. Moss green walls and wood flooring provide an appropriate backdrop.

Left: *Log walls are softened by colorful textiles hanging on racks. Both the quilt and pillows on the bed reinforce the color scheme selected to outfit this cozy sanctuary.*

Bottom Left: *Light yellow plasterboard walls and a vaulted ceiling visually expand this kids' bedroom and provide the perfect foil for red and blue bedding. Log beds echo the beauty of the great outdoors, as does the primitive dry sink now used as a nightstand. A rug with a Native American print, a painted chair, and assorted treasures on display enhance the woodland decor.*

Mountain and Woodland Retreats

Log walls and a red and green decorating scheme go hand in hand. In this mountain retreat, the pairing appears throughout the home, establishing a reassuring sense of continuity. Moreover, these colors surface in all sorts of unexpected places, providing a delightful sense of unpredictability and originality.

Left and Bottom Left: In the eat-in kitchen, forest green paint not only highlights the windows and doorway, but covers the entire ceiling as well. Providing a welcome counterpoint, red paint pitches in on the cabinetry and injects a vibrant note. But the kitchen's most distinctive feature is the vintage refrigerator, which has been decked out in a red, white, and green plaid finish.

Right: The bold color scheme continues to work its magic in the carefree living room. Everything about the decor—from the fish-back settee to the old pub sign—says that this getaway is a place to kick back and have some fun.

Wood flooring imbues a rustic home with natural color and texture. Myriad options make it almost difficult to select the perfect flooring; coloring, board widths, and upkeep all come under consideration. Hardwoods, such as oak, chestnut, maple, or cherry, can complement log walls by adding just a hint of contrast. Salvaged pine planking and other soft woods offer a warm, honey hue. For such hardworking areas as the kitchen, bath, entryway, and mudroom, tile, slate, or similar resilient flooring is frequently preferred for its low-maintenance nature. Bedrooms tend to require something a bit softer underfoot, so floors are often topped off with plain or patterned carpeting or room-size natural-fiber rugs.

Small cottage getaways require careful planning to maximize space. A big part of this design aspect involves providing out-of-the-way yet convenient storage. All those outdoor activities that are part of the attraction of having a woodland cottage come with paraphernalia. You need to find places for stowing sporting equipment, outdoor gear, and gardening tools. An enclosed back porch or a mudroom for stashing hiking boots, heavy jackets, fishing poles, backpacks, or ski equipment is ideal. Storage solutions for extra blankets, heavy sweaters, and other mountain-home necessities include everything from window seats to nooks with built-in shelves or cubbies.

Each room should have a focal point. In a rustic living room or great room, that focal point is, for the most part, the fireplace. On chilly autumn evenings or cool summer mornings, there's nothing like the warmth radiating from a log fire. And let's not forget a fire's power to capture attention and mesmerize, freeing the mind to wander. In mountain and woodland areas, hearths are usually made of river stone, site-specific rocks and boulders, granite, or occasionally brick. Modern cottages may also include a fireplace with a wood surround or simply a beautiful wood-burning stove. While some fireplaces are typical in size, others can be quite massive. Provide the perfect finishing touch by adding a log or half-rounded log mantel for the display of select nature-themed items—something as simple as a cluster of pinecones will have a strong decorative impact.

Above: *The trappings of a mountain getaway—sporting gear and warm outerwear—require storage space. This large entryway has been outfitted with a medley of hooks and racks for coats, shelves for hats and gloves, and an old church pew for comfort when putting on boots. Skis propped in the corner await the first snowfall.*

Opposite: *Not much else is called for in this living room where a massive stone hearth commands attention and infuses the space with a feeling of luxury. There is no artwork on the walls, nor is there a mantel for displaying bric-a-brac. The beauty of the logs and stones has resulted in a masterpiece needing little in the way of decorative accessories. To prevent the architectural elements from seeming too heavy, wicker furnishings introduce an airy quality.*

Several opportunities exist to create a stylistic, hallmark touch in the kitchen and bath. Custom-crafted cabinetry bearing beautiful wood tones, twig trim, birch bark–covered doors, or carved acorn pulls draws the woods indoors. To visually extend space in a smaller kitchen, stack dishes and the like in glass-fronted cabinets. Doing so will not only open up the room but will transform these necessities into decorative objects. Kitchen counters can be composed of rugged granite to reflect the setting, butcher block or a hardwood to recall the forest, or a less costly laminate that offers the look of stone or wood without the price tag.

Rustic Furnishings

A combination of craftsmanship, attention to detail, ingenuity, and reliance upon indigenous materials lies behind the furniture we recognize today as rustic. During the late nineteenth and early twentieth centuries, there was a growing demand for furnishings suited to the wilderness camps. As a result, guides, camp caretakers, and other untrained artisans began fashioning chairs, tables, cabinets, beds, and chests from trees. Twigs, branches, logs, burls, and bark all came into play in these creations.

By the 1890s, the need for Adirondack furniture, as it came to be known, was so great that several companies in the Midwest began turning out furniture crafted from hickory saplings. Appalachian artisans also left their mark by creating notable bentwood chairs and assorted pieces made from willow, rhododendron bushes, hickory, and laurel. Gypsies used willow to craft loop-back chairs, and throughout the American West and Southwest, cowboys and other untrained artisans fashioned furniture out of lodgepole pine, horns, and antlers. Today, these various types of furnishings can be used in a rustic cottage to achieve a natural look that echoes the outdoor setting.

If you decide to include vintage rustic-style pieces in your cottage decor, visit antiques dealers that specialize in this area. Inspect items carefully for any decay, rot, insect damage, loose joints, or sagging frames. While chairs, planters, benches, and tables are still fairly easy to locate, case pieces, dining tables, beds, and sideboards are rare and therefore can be quite costly. Thanks to an increasing demand for rustic pieces, many talented artisans have devoted their skills toward creating new furnishings in this style.

For a slightly more polished look, integrate Arts and Crafts furnishings with rustic-style pieces. Reflecting the rebellion against opulent home ornamentation and poor-quality mass-produced goods, Mission furnishings—often handcrafted of oak—are simple yet well designed. Don't worry if you can't get your hands on authentic antique pieces. Mission-style chairs, tables, settees, beds, chests of drawers, and so on are once again being crafted with quality materials and workmanship to meet the demand for straightforward furniture designs.

While a handsome table with hickory chairs may be perfect for camp dinners, when it comes to gathering in the living area or relaxing after a long hike, you're going to want the benefit of creature comforts. Toward this end, a rustic cottage calls for plump easy chairs and a sofa that you can melt into. Select roomy pieces that invite curling up or stretching out, and use hard-wearing

Opposite: *Achieving the best of both worlds, this contemporary kitchen has a rustic tone as well as a light and airy look. The effect was accomplished by incorporating cabinets that feature eye-catching twigwork and painting them white. A plank wall has also been painted white, causing the vintage architectural moldings, dishes, and cups on display to stand out and contribute artistic flair.*
Below: *Rustic furniture, much admired for its straightforward or intricate design, is the darling of woodland cottages and mountain camps. This particular bed, combining birch-bark logs and twigs, is a natural work of art.*

Mountain and Woodland Retreats

Opposite: *Relaxed ease in furnishings is paramount in a home designed for "getting away from it all," so rustic pieces should ideally be blended with sofas and easy chairs having deep cushions and soft curves. In this living room that recalls the American West, an oversize armchair and a sink-into couch offer the utmost in comfort, while a log end table complements a dazzling staircase.*

Above: *The Wild West may have been tamed but its spirit still soars in this log home designed for entertaining. A spacious open-living floor plan allows the kitchen and the dining area to share glorious views, while rounded logs, decorative river rocks, and a custom-crafted chandelier set the tone. In keeping with the rustic theme, log bar chairs line up at the counter for casual snacks and meals.*

fabrics—such as chenille, jacquard, corduroy, tapestry, denim, or leather—for upholstery. To provide visual interest, incorporate a sofa upholstered in a single hue that bears braiding in a contrasting color. A similar effect can be had by upholstering cushions in a patterned fabric. Checks, which combine easily with other designs—especially pictorials and floral prints—are an ideal choice due to their simplicity and vibrant colors. Plaids, Navajo prints, animal designs, and nature motifs can also be introduced to enhance rustic airs.

Wicker tables, sofas, chairs, and rockers can all make themselves at home in a rustic setting, especially when they display a natural finish or sport a coat of hunter green paint. Wicker's texture complements a back-to-nature decorating approach, but at the same time pieces are generally light and airy, which makes for refreshing contrast when blended with heavier wood pieces.

In a bedroom, a custom-crafted log or twig bed, an iron bed, or a painted wooden bed can become the focal point. Comb your attic for old dressers that can be brought back to life with paint, stain, or a thorough cleaning. For those who prefer new furniture, notable manufacturers offer lines that work well in casual and comfortable rustic environments.

Above: *Where mountain and woodland escapes are concerned, roughing it is definitely a thing of the past. Today, such getaways tend to boast artistic beauty, impressive craftsmanship, and yes, even solid comfort. Here a backdrop featuring barnwood doors and decorative twigwork is juxtaposed with an elegant roll-arm sofa that lends the room a slightly formal air.*

Left: *The elements in this seemingly simple bedroom have been carefully selected to achieve balance. A white painted wicker chair and a white quilt lighten up the wood tones of the backdrop and the log bed. As a result, the space projects a feeling of harmony—ideal for a peaceful night's rest.*

Let your rustic spirit soar when it comes time to outfit the kitchen and bath. A freestanding cupboard can be called upon to display collectibles or store kitchenware. A harvest table or a round table with rustic, painted, or wicker chairs will suit easy meals. In smaller spaces, a table with a vintage porcelain-enamel top may be just right for serving breakfast for two, and the bright and cheery colors found on many such pieces complement a woodland decor. Small tables or chairs can be put to work in the bathroom to hold toiletries or stacks of thick towels. Try hanging a birch bark–framed mirror above the sink for added rustic ambience.

Finishing Touches

A rustic retreat can become that special home away from home once you fill it with reflections of nature's beauty and the things you love. Decorative accessories may vary—they can imbue rooms with a subtle elegance for a sophisticated look or take a whimsical approach. The key lies in not decorating too seriously. Rooms should say something about the setting and the people who live there, but this kind of expressiveness doesn't happen overnight. Collections grow as new treasures are discovered.

Start by concentrating on elements that are both practical and decorative. Layer wood floors with rugs for warmth as well as color and texture. Faded oriental rugs with geometric designs, floral motifs, or striking center medallions will add a touch of refinement to a living area without detracting from the rustic mood. Along with pattern, either bright colors or muted shades can be selected to complement warm wood-paneled walls. Fur rugs have long been associated with interiors in the western states—a tradition that continues today. Smaller Navajo rugs and colorful rag rugs can be used in bedrooms, bathrooms, kitchens, or entryways. Keep handy doormats for wiping shoes and a bootjack for removing mud or dirt after trekking along mountain or forest trails.

In the secluded cottage, windows may be decorative in and of themselves, courtesy of their form and the

view that they frame. You may prefer to leave such windows bare. There are times, however, when some sort of window treatment will be desired to control lighting, provide a measure of privacy, or simply add style. When something a bit dressy is called for, floor-length drapes in a floral, checked, or nature-inspired design and hung on a decorative iron rod will speak volumes about rustic style. For a more casual approach, try simple curtains on iron, wooden, or twig rods. These can be used in virtually any room, as can your

Twin mirrors feature rustic trim that is echoed by the pulls on the vanity's cupboards and drawers. A Navajo rug takes the decorative tone up a notch, while a small stool stands ready to hold extra towels.

basic white roller, bamboo, or fabric shades. When your motive is purely decorative, consider hanging a valance in your favorite pattern or fabric.

When natural light is not enough, chandeliers or lamp bases crafted from horns or antlers, as well as twigwork and wrought-iron lamps, will pick up the slack and heighten the mood. Modern renditions of Arts and Crafts table lamps and lighting fixtures are also fitting. Look for mica lamps and hanging fixtures crafted with eye-catching metalwork. Try rawhide lampshades; glass shades with art glass inserts; parchment shades, which offer an aged look and occasionally decorative cutouts (such as leaves, bears, or deer); or hand-painted shades displaying leaves, acorns, pinecones, or animals.

Make sure you've got plenty of toss pillows on the sofa and a warm wool throw or two for curling up by the fire on cool nights. Print pillows and throws in either solid hues or checkered patterns are hallmarks of rustic style.

Artwork is another means of enhancing a rustic decor. Incorporate western art featuring cowboys, sunsets, and desert or mountain scenes. If something less regional is more to your liking, hang oil or watercolor paintings of mountains, forests, lakes, canoes, or even fishermen. Mount paintings in simple wood frames, or dress them up in gilt ones that will sparkle against the patina of a warm wood wall.

Decorative dishes—perhaps with a pinecone border, images of trees, or animal motifs—make a statement at meals and even throughout the day if they're on display on open shelving. Place wooden candlesticks and plaid napkins on the table, and put a bottle of wine in that old galvanized bucket to chill. Simple little details like these will make dinner gatherings more memorable.

Don't forget your special interests. The avid reader or history buff may collect books of regional interest, glossy photo-driven books that capture mountain ranges, forests, or lakes, or books that chronicle the development of resort areas. If there's no built-in shelves for these, stack them next to the sofa or atop a log coffee table.

Cottages and collecting seem to go hand in hand. While many accents are indicators of style, collections delve a little deeper to reveal personality. Your collections will give your cottage its individual character. And there are plenty of items associated with the woods and mountains, as well as life in those areas, that can serve as inspiration.

Perhaps vintage postcards are your thing. During the early twentieth century, many postcards were printed for rustic resorts and hotels and mountain vacation destinations. Celebrating the glory days of the great resorts, these vintage postcards can be framed and hung as artwork. Vintage botanical prints of leaves and ferns and prints of fish, birds, or game can be hung in groupings to convey a strong link to the outdoors. Intensify the connection to nature by showcasing these in twig or birch-bark frames.

Other items that come to mind are colorful trade blankets and camp blankets. Made of wool, the former were initially produced for Native American tribes in the northwest during the late 1800s and early 1900s. Trade blankets were manufactured in a variety of colors

Mountain and Woodland Retreats
129

Mountain and Woodland Retreats
130

Left: *When floor-to-ceiling windows bring the outdoor scenery into the decor, little is called for in the way of accessories. This log cabin, like many vacation homes, holds a mix of pieces; the goal is a comfortable space in which to relax and enjoy the view.*

Below: *White walls, log beams, and a stone floor form the setting for this room's flea-market finds. Assorted objects co-exist with a collection of mismatched chairs. The overall effect is one of relaxed comfort.*

Mountain and Woodland Retreats

Right: *This mountain retreat is filled with whimsical touches that exalt the surrounding wildlife and play up the Western locale. A bear stands ready to climb a treelike coatrack; a candle-holder boasts a macho cowboy; and a lamp with a cow-print shade features a base in the shape of a boot. A trade blanket draped across the leather sofa is great for snuggling under on cold, snowy days.*

Opposite Top: *An assortment of antique canteens hung from a peg rack projects a frontier spirit. Grouping such nostalgic items creates a focal point that celebrates days gone by.*

Opposite Bottom: *An artful display of old fishing lures, reels, and minnow buckets reveals a favorite pastime of the owners. Incorporating a collection that reflects your passion for a particular outdoor activity is one way of giving a cottage a personal stamp.*

with striped, geometric, and Navajo designs. Camp blankets differ from trade blankets on two fronts: they are made of cotton rather than wool and were aimed at the public in general. Sold through department stores between the 1930s and the 1950s, camp blankets were fashioned with Navajo designs as well as cowboy and Native American motifs. Today, both types of vintage blankets can provide warmth and color on sofas and beds. Those with worn areas or moth holes can be recycled into toss pillows or smaller lap throws.

Keep your eyes open for vintage fishing gear, such as wood or metal fishing lures, fishing flies with tinsel or colorful feathers, and galvanized minnow buckets. Fishing lures and flies can be displayed in slotted boxes, and those old minnow buckets can take on new life when filled with fresh flowers. Other sports-gear collectors hunt for old snowshoes, colorful wooden canoe paddles, and wooden skis. Any of these can be displayed above a mantel, hung on a wall, or even propped in a corner. Along the same lines, an old-fashioned wooden sled can become a decorative accent. For those with a strong interest in taxidermy, mounted deer, moose, and bears are still available at antiques shops and shows in mountainous and wooded regions.

To create a tabletop vignette, look to miniatures in the form of animals, log-home wood carvings, or rustic furnishings. These have been made for years as souvenirs for the tourist trade. Assemble a collection of dollhouse-size twig chairs or, perhaps, pint-size canoes.

Painted wood, wood-carved, and tin camp signs are other items that often appeal to those smitten by the rustic lifestyle. Advertising camps and cottage colonies, identifying rustic cafés and shops, or offering directions to some secret hideaway ("Greentree Camp Down the Road on the Left"), old signs are available in assorted shapes and sizes with hand-painted or machine-made designs. Display them on the screened porch, in the living room, or on a kitchen wall. Reproductions of these signs proliferate, so if you're looking for the real thing, visit noted dealers specializing in rustic memorabilia.

Opposite: *Spirited red and white checkered fabric and white painted furniture breathe life into this cottage kitchen.*

Above: *This rugged kitchen showcases a playful take on the traditional camp sign. Instead of a carved wooden board, the name of this wilderness getaway is featured on a hand-painted tile backsplash.*

CHAPTER FIVE

Outdoor Rooms

Come forth into the light of things,

Let Nature be your teacher.

—William Wordsworth, 1798

Whether you find yourself drawn to the majesty of the mountains, the power of the sea, the serenity of a crystal-clear lake, or the freedom of the wide-open countryside, you'll want to savor the natural beauty that surrounds you as much as possible. What better way to extend this pleasure than with an outdoor living space where you can soak in the natural landscape—the sights, the sounds, and the scents that speak to the spirit and soothe the soul.

Porches, Screened Rooms, Decks, and Patios

Depending upon the location, architectural style, and size of a cottage, it may have one or more outdoor living areas. A front porch—that classic spot for sitting a spell and taking in the view—often graces country retreats, from rustic mountain getaways to Victorian cottages by the sea. Much more than a transitional space between indoors and out, the front porch can be outfitted to function as a full-fledged open-air living room.

Other types of porches include side porches and wraparound ones. Both can easily be transformed into comfortable and inviting spaces to relax, entertain, read a good book, or dine alfresco. A wraparound porch may be preferable if a vacation home is sited where it can take advantage of more than one pleasing view. An L-shape porch can be furnished so that one side acts as a living room and the other as a dining space.

The nuts and bolts of porch design call for sturdy flooring, a porch overhang or roof, and a railing system. Depending on the architectural style, columns may enter into the mix. The porch of a log home in the middle of the

Previous Page: *The quintessential outdoor living space, the front porch affords hours of pleasure whether you're relaxing alone or enjoying the company of family and friends. As a transitional space between the outdoors and the interior, the porch serves up a warm welcome.*

Above: *Human artistry has been applied to natural elements, blending branches and pinecones into a fanciful fence.*

Opposite: *This lovely Victorian porch welcomes visitors with touches of blue that echo the sky and an exuberant mix of flowers.*

mountains may feature artistic twigwork or log trusswork in decorative trim and railings. In contrast, the porch of an old Greek Revival–style farmhouse may have an understated, almost spartan look with the exception of Doric columns used as support posts. No matter what the style, make sure that your porch is structurally sound, that pressure-treated lumber floors are properly maintained (usually with wood preservative or paint), and that railings are secure.

Porch flooring with a rugged wood finish complements a forest, lakeside, or mountain setting, but for homes situated in the open countryside or along the coast, a painted finish is usually preferred. Gray has long been the standard color for porch flooring, but a medium blue or green is certainly not out of the question. Look to the exterior colors of your home for inspiration. The porch ceiling can be treated to a wood finish, painted white, or decked out in a soft blue reminiscent of the sky.

In areas with year-round mild temperatures, porches can be built with slate, terra-cotta tile, or

ceramic tile flooring. These materials open up myriad options regarding color and pattern, so once again, look to the architectural design and exterior palette of your home to determine the best possible selections.

Screened porches combine the best of both worlds—the creature comforts of the indoors and the breathtaking beauty of nature. Some are designed from the get-go with screens and have a real roomlike appearance. These can be located at the side or back of the dwelling and can be quite large and elaborate. Other versions are merely front porches that were later fitted with screens to provide protection from weather and pesky insects. Indeed, this protection extends the amount of time that the space can be used. The transformation process is fairly simple, employing a series of framed screens designed to fit between porch posts. As with other types of outdoor living areas, screened porches are often poised to take advantage of a view and prevailing breezes. Investigate the various types of screening available to determine the quality level as well as the degree of transparency. After all, what good does it do you to have a screened porch if you can't see the surrounding scenery? Some owners go so far as to create a truly enclosed porch by using glazed inserts instead of screens to facilitate year-round use.

Flooring options in a screened room, depending upon location, include pressure-treated lumber, tongue-and-groove planking, stone, brick, tile, cement, and resilient flooring. Ceilings and trimwork can play up the outdoor nature of the space and manifest a rather rustic appearance with exposed wood beams and framing, or they can reflect the interior character of the room and display a more finished look.

Other outdoor living spaces—the open variety—include decks and patios. In most settings, these are located at the back or side of the house, though vacation homes on the water tend to place decks front and center to capitalize on spellbinding views. Decks built of pressure-treated lumber, redwood, or cedar are popular choices. Any decking material should be properly cared for to prolong its life. Routine maintenance entails periodic cleaning and finishing with a stain or preservative that has water-repellent properties.

Modern decks are a far cry from the simple rectangular versions that debuted a few decades ago. Multilevel decks, built-in planters and benches, and railings with sunburst designs are but a few of the creative options available. And because a deck can be tailored to blend with almost any house or site, there are few stylistic restrictions.

Consider the design and location of your cottage before planning a deck. Make a mental note of or actually list all the activities this feature will be used for. Then give thought to the deck's size and shape. If a railing is not necessary for safety, do you really want one? Will it just obstruct the view? If, on the other hand, a railing is definitely required (for an elevated building site or a deck that extends out over the water), explore the various options to maximize the view while still providing adequate protection.

Like a deck, a patio allows you to bask in the splendor of nature while keeping modern conveniences close at hand. One of the images that first comes to mind is that of a quaint little rose-covered cottage with a stone or brick path leading the way back to an intimate brick patio. While this is often the scenario, patios crafted with stone, tile, or cement are actually appropriate for many types of cottages, large and small. The Victorian cottage, the rural farmhouse, the English or French country retreat, and the seaside escape are all ideal vacation homes in which to incorporate a patio. Stone patios often suggest elegance and sophistication, while tile, with its earthy color and texture, exudes more rustic and European airs. The key is to design a patio that will meet your personal needs and encourage you to celebrate the outdoors.

Furnishing Outdoor Living Rooms

Your cottage is your special place—the refuge you return to time and time again to unwind and rejuvenate. With this in mind, shouldn't your outdoor living spaces be every bit as warm and inviting as the rooms inside your cottage?

Naturally, location and the particular type of outdoor living space will both have a big impact on the

furnishings you select. As you consider the myriad choices, think of the porch or patio as a family room and outfit accordingly. Will you be using the space simply as a gathering area, or do you want to be able to enjoy meals there? Will it be used in the evening? Choose furnishings that will provide loads of comfort for those who wish to spend hour upon hour in this outdoor space. Arrange furnishings to make the most of views as well as to facilitate conversation.

One of the most important aspects of outfitting an open, unprotected outdoor living space is the incorporation of weather-resistant furniture that will give you years of pleasure and use. Wicker is a favorite material for furnishing porches and decks, though you should make sure to use new pieces made with a weather-resistant, protective finish. Antique wicker furnishings should not be left outdoors, as they will not survive exposure to the elements. However, these older pieces have a lot to contribute to interior rooms, where they can create a breezy, gardenlike ambience. In woodland and lakeside settings, wicker pieces usually sport a natural or green painted finish to reflect the environment. In contrast, wicker furnishings set up on the front porch of a coastal retreat are often painted white to coincide with a lighter palette and decor. To maximize comfort, accessorize wicker chairs, sofas, rockers, settees, and ottomans with water-repellent cushions.

Opposite: *This spacious backyard deck includes a covered area for alfresco meals. Clay pots filled with geraniums reflect the beauty of the landscape just a stone's throw from the outdoor living room.*
Above: *At a charming cottage in the woods, forest green Adirondack furnishings and a rustic, willow chair are arranged for gathering. To ensure that wood furniture will last for years to come, clean and apply paint or wood preservatives as directed by manufacturers and store under cover during the winter months.*

Think muted floral patterns, solid colors, and checks for a woodland or lakeside milieu, and bright florals or casual stripes for coastal areas and farmhouse settings.

While new wicker furnishings are a popular choice, so too are wooden furnishings made of teak, redwood, cedar, or pressure-treated lumber. Designs range from contemporary to classic. For example, English garden–style furniture would be a most welcome addition to the cottage patio with English country airs. Wooden furniture can be painted, stained, or left alone to weather to one of various shades of gray depending upon the type of wood. Several notable furniture manufacturers have recently introduced lines of wooden outdoor furniture, and select items can also be found through mail-order catalogs

specializing in garden accessories. As with wicker chairs, invest in quality weather-resistant cushions intended for outdoor use.

One type of wooden furnishing in particular has become an icon of cottage life: the Adirondack chair. Possessing vast appeal, Adirondack chairs are just as likely to turn up on the deck of an oceanfront home as on the porch or lawn of a lakeside cabin or mountain retreat. Whether made of redwood, pine, or pressure-treated lumber, Adirondack chairs can be stained or allowed to weather to a natural gray. They can also be painted in a variety of cheerful hues or in the more traditional white or dark green.

In woodland and lakeside settings, front and screened porches often feature furnishings fashioned from twigs and logs. Establishing a strong link between

On this expansive front porch, matching twig chairs wear cheerful red and white cushions to provide comfort. Plants residing in a variety of containers, from tin pails to baskets, supply additional bursts of color.

the natural environment and the comforts of home, pieces made of these materials convey rustic style. Picture a wooden porch with a twig table surrounded by a pair of willow chairs and a willow settee outfitted with red and white checked seat cushions. This type of furniture can be obtained through artisans, select furniture manufacturers, and antiques dealers specializing in rustic decors. Just make sure that pieces used in outdoor areas are finished appropriately to stand up to weather conditions.

Should your cottage call for something a tad more elegant, there are numerous lines of decorative metal outdoor furnishings that will convey a polished appearance. Such pieces often bear enamel or paint to protect against rust. A painted white wrought-iron table and chair set might be just the thing to carry the romantic air of a country cottage decor onto the front porch or out to the patio. Aluminum furnishings, available in all sorts of styles and colored finishes, present another alternative. These lightweight yet durable pieces are a wise choice if you want to be able to move chairs and occasional tables around easily to take advantage of sunlight or shade or to accommodate company and activities.

Certain types of furnishings, such as a rocking chair, can really heighten your enjoyment of an outdoor space. Imagine the simple joy of rocking back and forth as you gaze out over a lake or study the mountains. Lining up several rockers on a front porch not only allows a number of family members and friends to experience this pleasure at the same time, but also creates a warm welcome and conveys a strong sense of hospitality. To express true laid-back cottage style, line up several different examples with paint-chipped or wood-tone finishes. Together, the various hues and stylistic variations will make quite the pretty picture. Look for vintage wooden rockers with rush-woven or wicker seats at antiques shops and shows, and always check carefully to make sure they're structurally sound. You can also purchase new rockers through department stores, furniture manufacturers, and mail-order catalogs that specialize in outdoor furnishings.

When it comes to decorating a porch in particular, don't overlook those items that convey the ultimate in porch style. A porch swing just big enough for two will

provide an intimate spot for deep talks on sunny afternoons and will fill the air with romance on hot summer nights. And what better place for that all-important afternoon nap than a hammock on the porch?

During the course of outfitting any type of outdoor space, make sure you've got a place to set cool drinks. Small tables can be scattered about for this purpose, or chairs can be grouped around an outdoor coffee table. Depending upon the size of the space, you may also want to include a table and chairs for dining. Remember that in a cottage setting, furnishings don't have to match. Seemingly disparate objects can be given a fresh coat of the same paint to create a surprisingly stylish setting. For example, an old wooden table painted white can be joined by a medley of chairs that have also been painted white to create a dining set— just make certain the chairs are of similar height. While the different styles will provide intriguing variety, the monochromatic scheme will tie all the pieces together. You could also create an appealing place to dine under the stars by surrounding a glass-top table with wicker chairs. On a patio, you might want to incorporate a table with an umbrella to block the sun during breakfast and lunch. Such a setup also makes for a shady spot for afternoon card games.

Rocking chairs are truly at home on a porch, where their soothing motion contributes to the restful ambience. Lined up to take in the lake view, these rockers—painted white to match the railing—offer a little piece of paradise.

Above and Right: *A beautiful table has been set for dinner in this airy glassed-in room. Clear blue stemware and white napkins with blue trim evoke images of being at the shore. Matching urns filled with seashells make fitting accents, bringing nature to the table. In the yard just beyond, that king of outdoor furnishings—the hammock— promises the utmost in relaxation. Accessorized with a blue pillow for daydreaming or catching an afternoon nap, this welcome feature speaks volumes about an easygoing lifestyle.*

Afternoon tea is served
on a shady brick patio.
Wicker chairs and a
decorative wirework settee
are gathered around a
table dressed up with a
festive cloth. The addition
of small pedestal tables
provides additional space
for drinks and snacks.
Despite the different
materials, the furnishings
look like they were made
to go together, thanks to a
white coat of paint.

Some furnishings that are particularly suited to a deck or patio as opposed to a porch include director's chairs, colorful "motel" chairs made of metal and sporting a retro look, and lightweight resin furnishings. Resin, a sturdy high-tech plastic, is amazingly durable and easy to clean. Some manufacturers are now making resin Adirondack-style chairs and assorted pieces that look like wicker. Most resin furniture comes in white, but color choices are expanding and now also include green and tan. Look for resin outdoor furniture at chain stores, department stores, and home building centers.

Please note: in cold-weather regions, outdoor furniture in general should be stored away for the winter months. Plastic covers suffice in warmer climates. Be sure to follow manufacturers' directions regarding periodic cleanings.

Accessories and Collectibles

Any outdoor living space should have all the comforts associated with a room where you entertain or simply enjoy spending time. While the surrounding natural scenery will no doubt take center stage, you want to create a welcoming, homey, and attractive setting from which to savor the view. Any casual, decorative style can easily be introduced to a porch, patio, or deck via select items that either serve a purpose or are simply whimsical accents.

The facade of a cottage usually makes a decorative contribution to the front porch. For instance, in the case of a woodland or mountain retreat, a stone, log, board-and-batten, or rough-cut lumber exterior makes a wonderful backdrop for porch furnishings. Add colorful red or dark green shutters—perhaps ones sporting pine tree, pinecone, or animal cutouts—and you'll imbue your outdoor sanctuary with notable rustic style. Build on that by adding Arts and Crafts–style or black wrought-iron sconces on either side of the front door.

If you want to be able to use your porch in the evening, you'll need to install light fixtures. Lighting not only provides a practical service, but can affect the ambience as well. Options include both wall and

Right: *Boating and fishing are no doubt favorite pastimes at this wooded, lakeside retreat. As a purely whimsical touch, old oars have been used to create a folk-art type pole suggesting the pleasures of the day. After the canoe is docked and the fishing gear stored, drinks can be served on the inviting brick patio.*

Right Bottom: *This custom-crafted iron lighting fixture illuminates the front porch of log cabin. Keeping the wooded landscape in mind, the glass inserts have been designed with pinecone motifs. Small details such as this lend outdoor living spaces all the charm and warmth associated with interior rooms.*

Opposite: *An enclosed porch with French doors, a skylight, and decorative lattice ceiling panels is the perfect spot to host a brunch. Doors are opened wide to invite in gentle breezes as guests dine at tables bedecked with cheerful textiles. With fresh flowers, lush greenery, and picture-perfect table settings, the atmosphere rivals any country dining room.*

hanging fixtures, which come in a variety of different materials. Enhance these with lanterns and citronella candles to set a peaceful, romantic mood.

Often, a cottage will have been named by its current or previous owners. The dwelling's title may simply take the form of the family name, as in Smith's Cottage, or it can reflect the natural setting, such as Wildwood. What better way to welcome family and guests than with an identifying plaque prominently displayed on the front porch? Such a sign can boast bark and twigwork, hand-painted lettering on stone, or carved wood lettering and painted scenic designs. Hand-painted tiles are a popular choice for cottages by the sea.

Adding comfort and beauty means accessorizing porch chairs and other seating with not only plump cushions, but colorful pillows and throws as well. For a rustic decor, Navajo prints, checks, and deep-colored floral patterns are an excellent choice. Stripes and large, bright floral designs, on the other hand, are better suited to a seaside escape or a farmhouse in a rural setting. Depending upon location, you may want to install bamboo or matchstick blinds to filter bright light. Canvas shades will also provide respite from the hot sun.

The rustic front porch is an ideal place to hang a patriotic flag, an old paint-chipped canoe paddle, a pair of retired snowshoes, or a seasonal wreath. A large basket or wrought-iron stand can be placed on the porch beside the front door to hold logs for the living room fireplace. Not only is this a convenient way to keep a supply of chopped wood close at hand, but it also contributes a decorative touch. At the shore, a porch might be accessorized with nautical paraphernalia punctuating the wall and woven baskets of seashells, coral, and driftwood perched on tables and plant stands or resting on the floor. And in any setting, wind chimes will delight the ears and soothe the soul.

No porch would be complete without flowers or greenery. Hanging plants, such as ferns or ivy geraniums, are ideal for their lush color and summertime beauty. If there are other cottages nearby and you want to create a little privacy, mount window boxes on the

Left: *A screened room located apart from the main cottage yet connected by a breezeway serves as a quiet refuge. Wicker furnishings have been arranged to make the most of the water view.*

porch railing and fill them with tall blooming plants—just make sure they don't block your view of the landscape beyond. The porch floor and steps can play host to clay pots (with drip saucers) filled with colorful annuals, such as petunias or geraniums, or even small shrubs. If you have a ledge that's wide enough, go ahead and line it with a few potted plants. Wooden tubs made of cedar or redwood also make excellent containers and show off a great deal of natural, rugged texture.

The screened porch takes outdoor decorating to the next level, especially in those areas where the space can be enjoyed all year long. Give thought to using natural-fiber rugs, colorful rag rugs, or weather-resistant room-size carpeting. Rugs can be color-coordinated to match fabrics on furniture, throw pillows, or decorative window valances, a look that's especially appealing in a rural cottage or farmhouse. Outfit the screened room with roll-up shades to control sunlight. Besides bamboo shades, woven grass shades might appeal to those in seaside retreats. For nighttime comfort, include a

Above: *A treasure trove of decorative accessories sets a jovial tone in this screened porch. A striped rag rug softens plank flooring and contributes to the lived-in feel of the space.*

Right: *This rustic porch greets visitors with an eye-catching vignette composed of an old paint-chipped farm table and other icons of country life. A woven basket filled with flowers, herbs hung up to dry, and corn waiting to be shucked all pay homage to the bounty of nature.*

Opposite: *Steps leading up to the porch of a wood-land cottage extend a cheerful welcome, courtesy of clay pots filled with blooming plants. Even a colorful enameled coffee pot gets in on the act with its display of black-eyed Susans. Container garden-ing is the perfect way to bring color onto the porch.*

tabletop lamp or two, recessed lighting, or the all-important ceiling fan with lights.

Personalize the screened room. If boating is your passion, say it loud and clear. Hang a seascape on the interior wall or line up favorite boating collectibles on a display shelf. If you're a devoted gardener, turn the screened room into a garden room and fill it with shade-loving plants, such as ivy or begonias, housed in assorted clay pots or old enamelware containers. Complement your natural accessories with floral pil-lows and tablecloths. At mealtime, set the table with theme dishes and stemware—for instance, blue glass-ware that echoes the sea for a home at the shore, pot-tery with a pinecone motif for a refuge in the moun-tains, or china with petite floral sprays for the cottage surrounded by fields.

Decks and patios can be minimally decorated to pay homage to a striking view or embellished with myriad accessories that create their own scenic beauty. First, look at practical considerations. For protection from less-than-ideal weather or direct sunlight, is a canvas awning called for or will umbrellas do? Is priva-cy an issue? If so, decorative lattice panels could be the solution. Do you plan to entertain a great deal? A gas grill or built-in barbecue will make for easy meals. If the lighting fixtures attached to the house don't provide adequate nighttime illumination, you may want to install landscape lights around the deck or patio. As with a porch, it is always a good idea to have citronella candles on hand, as well as decorative lanterns or votives that can be scattered about.

Like other outdoor areas, decks and patios can benefit from flowers and greenery. Built-in planters, decorative metal or wicker plant stands, and an array of decorative pots can all be filled with summer blooms and sprinkled about the deck. Flowers can be color-coordinated with fabrics used on seat cushions or selected simply to provide beautiful contrast. Picture the seaside escape with weathered gray shingles, white trim, and a deck outfitted with white wicker furniture and clay pots filled with bright red geraniums. Such a simple natural accessory will make a powerful state-ment, proving that less is indeed sometimes more.

Last but not least, consider ways to enhance the view from your outdoor living space. For example, you might want to situate a birdfeeder within easy sight of your porch or patio to attract some delightful feathered friends. And keep binoculars close at hand to extend the boundaries of your viewing pleasure.

Cottage Gardens

Gardening has moved to the forefront of our favorite pastimes. Considered a leisure activity by many, plant-ing and tending a garden can be a perfect way to relax, feel connected to nature, and create something beauti-ful. Even if you don't stay the whole season in your vacation retreat, returning on weekends means you can still plan a relatively easy-care garden that will give you hours of pleasure and satisfaction.

First things first: a small potting shed, a potting room off the kitchen, or a gardener's workbench on the deck or patio is optimal for rounding up the tools of the gardening trade, such as small shovels, spades, forks, watering cans, clay pots, gloves, garden stakes, baskets for cutting flowers, seed containers, and so on. Even this functional workstation can be an attractive addition

Right: *This homey potting shed is a gardener's dream come true. Dressed with sunny yellow walls and equipped with all the tools of the trade, the space becomes a peaceful haven for those with a passion for plants.*

Opposite Top: *A compact porch can still be highly hospitable, as evidenced by this snug yet delightful example. A narrow table slides up against the edge of the porch, where it serves as a space-efficient buffet, and a small painted iron table pitches in as an extra resting spot for food and drink. Tall potted plants and a bamboo shade filter sunlight so that early risers can linger over juice and coffee.*

Opposite Bottom: *A seaside garden enhances the view from a sweeping wraparound porch. Notice how the curve of the porch echoes that of the shore.*

to the cottage given the various shapes and textures of objects called into use.

The garden itself, located at the front, side, or rear of the cottage, can be an informal flower bed, a rock garden, a rose garden, an herb garden, or perhaps something a bit more formal with a clipped hedgerow and garden paths or paved areas. Garden accoutrements such as arbors, decorative arches, or gazebos can convey style via the materials they're constructed from—for example, twigs for a rustic look or white painted lumber for fetching cottage appeal. Lattice panels, picket fences, ornate iron fencing, and rock walls can be incorporated as needed to define property or space and to add privacy.

Ideally, a flower garden combines perennials with colorful annuals. Such perennials as daylilies and hostas have long been called upon to give a garden height and rich, green color. Myriad annuals, including pansies, marigolds, petunias, lilies of the valley, and coralbells can be planted seasonally for color, shape, and texture. Unless you're an experienced gardener, check with a local nursery to determine the best sun- or shade-loving plants for your particular garden site.

The garden is highly decorative in and of itself, but adornments don't stop with flowers. Garden accessories that contribute charm and cottagelike appeal include a birdbath or birdhouse, a garden bench so that you may sit and enjoy your handiwork, a trellis for climbing vines alongside the house, and a fountain to give the garden pleasant sound effects. The list can go on and on—just use your imagination and your own sense of style.

What to do if natural terrain prohibits a garden? Create a container garden. Pots large and small can be used to plant flowers, herbs, and even vegetables, and can then be grouped on the patio, on the deck, or in the yard. Terra-cotta pots are always good choices, but don't limit yourself—many cottage accessories, from baskets to old tinware, make useful and charming planters. A cottage garden, whether potted or planted in the ground, provides a wonderful connection to nature—the essence of cottage living.

Source Directory

Furnishings, Accessories, and Interior Design

Adirondack Country Store
252 North Main Street
P.O. Box 210
Northville, NY 12134
518-863-6056
www.adirondackcountrystore.com

Adirondacks Rustics Gallery
RR1 Box 88
Charley Hill Road
Schroon Lake, NY 12870
518-532-9384
www.adkrustics.com

Adirondack Store
109 Saranac Avenue
Lake Placid, NY 12946
518-523-2646
and
90 Main Street
New Canaan, CT 06840
203-972-0221

Barry Friedman
P.O. Box 55492
Valencia, CA 91385
805-255-2365
Specializes in rustic antiques, including Navajo blankets.

Beach Cottage Linens
225 Redfern Village
St. Simons Island, GA 31522
877-451-6994
www.beachcottagelinens.com

Be-Speckled Trout
422 Hudson Street
New York, NY 10014
212-255-1421
Specializes in fishing collectibles.

The Chuctanunda Antique Company
One Fourth Avenue
Amsterdam, NY 12010
518-834-3983
www.enameledware.com
Specializes in vintage French and European enamelware.

Country Curtains
The Red Lion Inn
Route 7
Stockbridge, MA 01262
800-876-6123

Evergreen House Interiors
71 Main Street
Lake Placid, NY 12946
518-523-4263

French Country Living
10205 Colvin Run Road
Great Falls, VA 22066
703-759-2245
Specializes in French country–style decorative accessories.

L. & J.G. Stickley, Inc.
Stickley Drive
P.O. Box 480
Manlius, NY 13104
315-682-5500
Specializes in Arts and Crafts/Mission oak furniture.

Laura Ashley Home Collection
1300 MacArthur Boulevard
Mahwah, NJ 07430
800-223-6917
Specializes in fabrics and wallpapers for an English country–style decor.

Laura Fisher/Antique Quilts & American
1050 Second Avenue, Gallery #84
New York, NY 10022
212-838-2596

L.L. Bean Home Furnishings
L.L. Bean, Inc.
Freeport, ME 04033
800-221-4221
www.llbean.com

Maine Cottage Furniture, Inc.
P.O. Box 935
Yarmouth, ME 04096
207-846-1430

Marine Arts Gallery
135 Essex Street
P.O. Box 818
Salem, MA 01970
508-745-5000
Specializes in vintage drawings and paintings of marine subjects.

McGuire Furniture Company
151 Vermont Street
San Francisco, CA 94103
800-662-4847
www.mcguirefurniture.com

Mica Lamp Company
520 State Street
Glendale, CA 91203
818-241-7227

Moose America
73 Main Street
P.O. Box 7
Rangeley Lakes, ME 04970
207-864-3699
Specializes in rustic furniture and accessories.

Moose Creek Limited
1592 Central Avenue
Albany, NY 12205
518-869-0049
and
Moose Creek Limited North
10 State Route 149
Lake George, NY 12845
518-745-7340
www.moosecreekltd.com

Old Hickory Furniture
403 South Noble Street
Shelbyville, IN 46176
800-232- 2275
Specializes in rustic furniture.

Pier 1 Imports
Call 800-44PIER1 for store locations.
www.pier1.com

The Ralph Kylloe Gallery
P.O. Box 669
Lake George, NY 12845
518-696-4100
Specializes in rustic furniture and camp
accessories.

Stein Mart
Call 888-STEINMART for store locations.
www.steinmart.com

Taos Furniture
1807 Second Street Studios
Santa Fe, NM 87505
800-443-3448\
www.taosfurniture.com
Specializes in western rustic furniture.

Yowler & Shepps Stencils
3529 Main Street
Conestoga, PA 17516
717-872-2820
Specializes in decorative stencils.

Home Building and Design

Adirondack Design Assoc.
62 Livingston Street
Rhinebeck, NY 12572
914-876-2700
www.adkgreatcamps.com

Deck House, Inc.
930 Main Street
Acton, MA 01720
800-727-3325
www.deckhouse.com

Northeastern Log Home
Route 302
Groton, VT 05046
800-992-6526

Northern Design & Building Assoc., Ltd.
P.O. Box 47
Hudson Falls, NY 12839
800-576-0557
www.northerndesign.com
Specializes in design home kits.

Tennessee Log Homes
P.O. Box 865
Athens, TN 37371
www.tnloghomes.com/tnlog

Wisconsin Log & Cedar Homes
2390 Pamperin Road
Green Bay, WI 54313
800-844-7970

Outdoor Furnishings and Decorative Accessories

Brown Jordan
9860 Gidley Street
El Monte, CA 91731
818-443-8971
Specializes in aluminum, wrought-iron, resin
weave, and teak furniture.

Ficks Reed Company
4900 Charlemar Drive
Cincinnati, OH 45227
513-985-0606
Specializes in wicker furniture.

The Lane Company, Inc.
Venture Division
Box 849
Conover, NC 28613
800-750-5236
Features a line of "Weather Master" wicker
furniture.

Lloyd Flanders
3010 10th Street
P.O. Box 550
Menominee, MI 49858
906-863-4491
Specializes in all-weather wicker furnishings.

Smith & Hawkin
800-981-9888
Call for catalog of furnishings and garden
accessories.

PHOTO CREDITS

©Phillip Beaurline: pp. 2, 77 right, 80 top, 85 top, 90–91, 96–97, 152

©Steven Brooke Studios: pp.18, 24–25, 26–27, 28, 30–31, 36-37(designed by Armando Valdes, Architect), 115 top, 146–147 (designed by Ton Luyk)

©Phillip Clayton-Thompson: p. 66 top (styling by Donna Pizzi)

Elizabeth Whiting Associates: p. 41 ©Brian Harrison

©Tony Giammarino: pp. 10, 33 top, 33 bottom, 42 (designed by Christine McCabe), 48, 75 (Buffalo Springs Herb Farm, Raphine, VA), 93 top, 105, 151 right (designed by Thomas Greene)

©Tria Giovan: pp. 15, 19, 39 right, 79 top, 79 bottom, 124 top, 131

©Jessie Walker Associates: pp. 11, 31 right, 32 (Hackley/Lang Associates), 50 (Hackley/Lang Associates)top, 69 (Hackley/Lang Associates), 88 top, 95, 97 right, 113 right, 148 top, 149, 153

©David Livingston: p.34

©Keith Scott Morton: pp. 26 left, 43 top, 47 right, 52 left

©Eric Roth: pp. 12, 20, 35, 36 left, 40, 45, 73, 78, 88 bottom, 94, 99 bottom, 111, 120, 134, 137, 140, 141, 143, 155 top

©Samu Studios: p. 83 right (designed by Ruth Sommers Design)

©Brad Simmons Photography: pp. 5, 9, 55, 56, 57, 60, 61, 62, 64–65, 66 bottom, 67, 76–77, 80 bottom, 85 bottom, 86 bottom, 87, 93 bottom, 98, 99 top, 100, 101, 102, 104, 110, 114, 115 bottom, 116 top, 116 bottom, 116–117, 118, 119, 121, 122, 123, 125, 128 bottom, 129, 130, 133 top, 133 bottom, 135, 138, 139, 142, 148 bottom, 154, 155 bottom

©Tim Street-Porter: pp. 29, 43 bottom (designed by Andrew Virtue), 81, 84 (designed by Barbara Barry), 86 top (designed by Jarrett Hedborg; painted surfaces by Nancy Kintisch), 100, 132, 144 left, 144-145 (designed by Stephen Brady)

©Brian Vanden Brink: pp. 6–7, 13 (John Silverio, Architect), 16, 17 top, 17 bottom, 21, 38–39, 46–47 (Stephen Blatt, Architects), 49 (John Silverio, Architect), 50 bottom (John Silverio, Architect), 51, 52–53, 58–59, 63 (Scholz & Barclay, Architects), 65 right, 68 (Chris Campbell, Architect), 70–71, 71 right, 74 (Centerbrook Architects), 82–83, 89, 92, 103, 107, 108 (Bullock & Co. Log Homes), 109 (Bullock & Co. Log Homes), 112–113 (Stephen Blatt, Architects), 124 bottom (Rob Whitten, Architect), 126–127, 128 top (Stephen Blatt, Architects), 150–151 (Rob Whitten, Architect)

©Dominique Vorillon: pp. 22–23, 24 left